Praise For
The People Keeper

"*The People Keeper* is easy reading, yet a highly informative guide to recruiting, and more importantly, retaining *people*. I will put the ideas to use with our employees and my management staff."

Jim Lindemann, Chairman & CEO
Emerson Motor Company (and Executive V.P., Emerson Electric)

"Timely, relevant, and a must read. Writing with remarkable clarity Mark Holmes tackles the number one issue facing corporate America today, strengthening their magnet to attract and retain people."

Mark Conklin, Internal Consultant-Field Operations
Chick-fil-A, Inc.

"Mark Holmes' book *The People Keeper,* is very timely, the issue of employee retention is a very real concern facing Corporate America today. The book will have great appeal to, and should be a must read for every business owner and manager!"

John Topping, Jr., Director of Marketing
Big Rock Sport Group (Henry's, All Sports, Avis Sports)

"In the dotcom world, attracting and keeping good employees is 'the' challenge. *The People Keeper* should be a huge winner and extremely useful by leaders at *all* levels."

Doug Ausbury, CEO
Intrapromote

"Now and in the future, service companies must differentiate themselves from their competition by offering their employees more than just a job. *The People Keeper* teaches managers how to make their business a place that the best employees never leave because they actually enjoy going to work each day!"

Mark Vanase, Market Manager of Franchise Operations
ServiceMaster Clean

"Applying these ideas can lead to a positive workplace where best employees thrive. I know my company's work culture and employee satisfaction have improved as we have applied more of Mark's People Keeper methods!"

Brian Hammons, President
Hammons Products Company

"Mark Holmes has produced a fascinating book that answers the # 1 question on the minds of business leaders throughout the world today — how do I keep my best employees? Read it, apply the principles, and succeed!"

Brian Molitor, Author
The Power of Agreement

"An issue every business struggles with, including our own, is how to attract and retain quality employees. *The People Keeper* has great appeal to business. Personally, I'd want to get a copy in the hands of every manager in our company."

Nathan Long, Director of Customer Service,
Tracker Marine

"Holmes has written a powerful book that's easy to read and yet filled with wisdom. Most organizations seem to pay attention to turnover and retention issues only when they find themselves already immersed in a crisis. By then it's too late. This book shows how to keep that from happening from the start!"

B. Douglas Clinton, CPA, Ph.D
Northern Illinois University

THE PEOPLE KEEPER

How Managers Can Attract, Motivate And Retain Better Employees

MARK HOLMES

THE PEOPLE KEEPER

How Managers Can Attract, Motivate And Retain Better Employees

MARK HOLMES

Advance Mark Publishing

THE PEOPLE KEEPER
How Managers Can Attract, Motivate and Retain Better Employees

Published by: Advance Mark Publishing
Springfield, Missouri

Advance Mark Publishing
P.O. Box 3175
Springfield, MO 65808

Hardcover ISBN: 0-9643828-4-9
Softcover ISBN: 0-9643828-5-7

Library of Congress Cataloging-in-Publication Data

Holmes, Mark, 1957-
    The people keeper : how managers can attract,
motivate and retain better employees / Mark Holmes. —
1st ed.
    p. cm.
    LCCN: 00-191015
    ISBN: 0-9643828-5-7

    1. Employee retention. 2. Personnel management.
3. Employees—Recruiting.   I. Title.

HF5549.5.R58H65 2001   658.3'14
                              QBI01-200202

Cover design and layout: Ad Graphics, Inc., Tulsa, OK
Printed in the United States of America

For more information about *THE PEOPLE KEEPER*
Books in volume discount, Training Materials or Consulting:
www.thepeoplekeeper.com
800-841-8540

CONTENTS

PREFACE

People want and need to feel appreciated and valued in the workplace. They want to be recognized for their contributions and they want to work in a positive atmosphere. They want to work for amicable managers who give regular feedback, are sensitive to their needs, and value their contributions. They want more than just a paycheck.

Managers want to attract better employees. They want to get the most from their efforts and they want consistent performance. They want to retain top performers and reduce the heavy cost of turnover. They want a day's work for a day's pay. Giving employees what they want while satisfying the needs of managers isn't difficult. The driving theme of this book is just that — *the desire of managers to attract and retain better employees is readily fulfilled when the fulfillment of employees is readily desired.*

Unfortunately, in today's business environment few employers or managers really pay enough attention to what employees want. Too few prioritize the satisfaction of employees like they do the satisfaction of their customers.

Consequently the turnover turnstile is constantly in motion as new employees replace experienced employees who depart for the lure of greener pastures. Much of this loss is unnecessary and can be easily prevented.

Managers who motivate and retain better employees will definitely enjoy the advantages of seasoned experience and enhanced core competencies, such as increased profitability and strengthened viability. They raise their ability to change quickly while increasing customer satisfaction. They attract select employees and create word-of-mouth hiring because they develop a First-Choice Employer reputation.

This book will help managers keep their stars on *their* team. These ideas will rejuvenate the work experience and supply proven ways to increase motivation and retention without enlarging the paycheck.

ACKNOWLEDGMENTS

This book began as I prepared to speak on motivating employees at Chick-fil-A's corporate convention a year ago. But the insistence of Mark Conklin and several store managers (operators) later convinced me that I should also address the issues of attracting and retaining better employees. I am thankful for their persuasion and Mark's enthusiastic support.

Special thanks goes to three of my former bosses. Robert Davis created a most positive and stimulating work environment. Alvin Rohrs at Students In Free Enterprise always operated with a clear vision and demonstrated a value for top performers that any professional longs for. Both men were great examples of People Keepers. I also thank another boss, who will go unnamed, he provided me with the *worst* example of how to manage and motivate people. No one welcomes working for a boss like him, but I am wiser for it.

My mom taught me the value of loving and respecting all people. Her perspective came from my granddad, Jesse Shands. If he were alive, he'd still be a People Keeper at his little café in Missouri, and he'd still be serving poor families with free food. Such caring is a guide for and in all I do.

I was blessed with a gem of an editor, Christine Gonzales. Her vast skills enriched my words and thoughts. Jim Weems is an awesome cover designer, and I was fortunate to have the benefit of his talents.

I have a great wife and two children, and my life is quite fulfilled with them as a vital part of all I endeavor.

CHAPTER ONE

The Original People Keeper

The old archaeologist lingered over the hole where he'd been working on hands and knees for two days. He bent back down and gently slipped a hand underneath the heavy stone tablet. With a slight turn he wedged his fingers further beneath the corner and then slowly attempted to lift it out.

Feeling the aged stone crumble slightly, he abruptly stopped and withdrew his hand until the tablet rested again on its familiar sandy home of nearly two thousand years.

Over the next several hours the old man tried every extraction technique known, but nothing could prevent further damage to the nearly two-inch thick tablet.

Since he couldn't physically remove the tablet without possibly destroying it, he began concentrating on how to best transcribe the message.

The old man bustled down the knoll to his tent. He unpacked the carbon markers and special parchment paper that he would use to reproduce the symbols. Carefully rubbing the tablet over and over again with the carbon markers, the old man made sure that each mark was copied completely.

Finished, the archaeologist made the long journey home with an excitement equaled only to his first discovery. It took the old man the two remaining years of his life to trace and authenticate the tablet's secrets...

THE TABLET'S SECRET

Once there was a young leader who was to lead his captive kinsmen to freedom and to a land rich with food and natural resources. But he lacked wisdom and soon was frustrated by the rebelliousness and lack of unity among his people. The young leader wanted to quit.

Fortunately, his father-in-law noticed his frustration and offered him great wisdom. In a matter of months, the young leader was able to turn the situation around, using his father-in-law's advice. He skillfully united his kinsmen and led them successfully through hardship, life-threatening events and numerous enemy encounters to possess a rich land they could claim as their own. The young leader became legendary as a motivator and leader. Kings from all over the world sought his wisdom and other nations aspired to join him. The young leader was encouraged to record his wisdom of leading people on a tablet. This extraordinary information was recorded in the form of the Five Tenets.

The old man finished transcribing the last page and placed it in the leather journal along with the other typewritten pages for safe keeping. He called his only son to his bedside, there he bequeathed the secrets of the tablet just before his death.

Sawyer Marion, the archaeologist's son, was a successful business owner and executive. Over the next 30 years, with the secrets of the tablet put to work at his own company, his wealth and fame soared. Additionally, Sawyer had been careful to keep current by researching everything he could find on employee retention and motivation, adding sparingly to the tablet's original Five Tenets.

Managers and leaders from all over now pursued Sawyer's advice. His company had also earned a reputation as being the best place to work — if you could get hired. According to local lore, once you worked for Sawyer, you'd never want to leave.

He was asked once, "What do you call this unique philosophy of yours, so simple in form but so powerful in results?"

His patient answer was always the same:

"The People Keeper."

CHAPTER TWO

The Mentor Invests Himself

Two hundred miles away, Jesse sat thinking in his spacious office located above the massive showroom business he'd grown from a small metal building. Twenty years of his business life had flown by fast.

But he faced a crisis in his career. He had never had so much trouble attracting and keeping better employees. The scarcity of quality employees was catching up with him. Every business professional he knew was grappling with the same issue ....

... how to attract and keep better employees.

He picked up the phone to dial Sawyer, his mentor, knowing that Sawyer would have the advice he needed, he *always* did.

Sawyer patiently listened to his problem and graciously invited Jesse for a visit. He said he wanted to share something that he had never passed on before, at least in its entirety. He said that the People Keeper was a positive way of relating to employees, and that he personally attributed his own company's success to its wisdom.

The more Sawyer shared about the People Keeper, the more Jesse knew that it was exactly what he and his managers needed right now.

"I can't wait to learn more about the People Keeper," Jesse said.

"Great, I'll put you on hold and you can work out the schedule with Anne," Sawyer said.

Sawyer hung up the phone realizing now that he wanted Jesse, his long-time protégé, to possess the secrets of the People Keeper. He wanted Jesse to share the power of the secrets with others.

CHAPTER THREE

Becoming A People Keeper

"Hello Anne, you're as lovely as ever," Jesse said while handing her the fresh rose he had bought only a few blocks from Sawyer's facilities.

"Just look at you Jesse, you're still a charmer and a gentleman," Anne answered with a blush. "Go right on in. I've not seen him this excited about anything in some time," she whispered as he stepped in.

"Jesse," Sawyer called out with delight, looking up form his thick-rimmed glasses. Limping a bit, he walked around the desk and thrust his right hand out for a quick hand shake followed by a big welcome hug.

Jesse noticed Sawyer's limp and his gnarled hand as he withdrew from the hug and headed back to his chair. Sawyer's once jet-black hair was quite gray, and arthritis had left its cruel signs on both hands.

Sawyer motioned for Jesse to take a seat and wasted no time getting started. "Well, what's the first thing that you want to know about being a People Keeper?"

"I was hoping to find out why being a People Keeper is so important to your company?"

"If you work here as a manager, you must become a People Keeper, it's that simple," Sawyer emphasized, handing Jesse a laminated card.

"What's this?" he asked surprised.

"It's a reminder of the reasons why we believe that it's critical to become a People Keeper," answered Sawyer.

Jesse read the reminder tool:

FOUR REASONS WHY WE MUST BE PEOPLE KEEPERS:
■■■■■■■■■■■■■■■■■■■■■

1. When you lose a valued employee, you lose more value than you think.

2. Pay won't make them stay!

3. Attracting better employees will only get harder, so invest *now* in keeping the valued employees that you already have.

4. It pays to be a First-Choice Employer.

When Jesse finished reading, he looked up and locked eyes with Sawyer for a moment, sensing that the enthusiasm he saw was real.

"What do you mean by, 'First-Choice Employer?'" asked Jesse as he pointed to the fourth reason.

"Being a First-Choice Employer means that your company earns the privilege of being the first employment choice of potential employees, while remaining the first employment choice of your current associates," Sawyer explained.

"How does a company become a First-Choice Employer?" asked Jesse.

Sawyer had a plan for Jesse's learning, and he knew that as the week progressed Jesse would learn all the secrets of being a People Keeper and a First-Choice Employer. But for now, Sawyer only said, "When you become a company of People Keepers only then will you become a First-Choice Employer."

"You really believe that the People Keeper principles are the right thing to do for your company, don't you?"

"Yes," said Sawyer, "I know it's the right thing for my company because it's the right thing for my employees. When you realize that losing a valued employee can cost up to 200 percent of their annual salary and benefits, you should be highly motivated to try to keep every good employee you've got." Then Sawyer made a key point that Jesse wrote down:

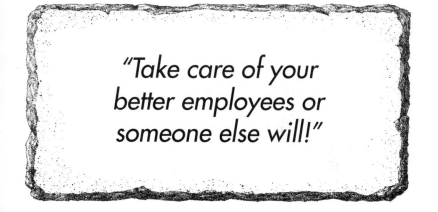

"Take care of your better employees or someone else will!"

"So, the People Keeper is a good strategy for keeping other employers away from your better employees," Jesse broke in. "And it's the right thing to do financially for the company."

"Right," Sawyer said. "The intelligent thing to do is to make your company so appealing to work at that better employees don't want to look around. That way you lower turnover and stop losing so much money on replacing better employees. For example, did you know that if your company loses an employee that makes let's say $30,000.00 annually, that can run you $60,000.00 in real replacement costs?"

"I don't get that at all," Jesse said. "How does turnover cost up to 200 percent of an employee's compensation?"

"Maybe this will explain it," answered Sawyer as he located a guide sheet and handed it to Jesse.

"Basically you have two costs, replacement costs and intellectual capital costs. 'Replacement Costs' are the normal costs of running ads, interviewing time, new employee training, new employee compensation package and so forth. All of that can quickly add up to one and a half to two times compensation," he said.

"Then if you add the 'Intellectual Capital Costs,' such as lost experience, lost proficiency and even lost business that results from losing a better employee, the real costs can exceed double their compensation," Sawyer said as he watched Jesse take notes.

EMPLOYEE REPLACEMENT COSTS
■■■■■■■■■■■■■■■■■■■■■■■■■

Replacement Costs:

- Recruiting (advertising cost, time, resources)
- Interviewing time
- Hiring (support costs, employee uniforms, etc.)
- New employee training
- Moving expenses
- Compensation differences (higher pay, or more hours to replace employee)

Intellectual Capital Costs:

- Loss of productivity until new employee is proficient
- Loss of hard to replace skills, knowledge or experience
- Loss of problem solving abilities
- Loss of business
- Loss of morale (co-workers impacted negatively by the loss)
- Loss of other employees (co-workers who leave from the ripple effect)

"These costs really add up quick," Jesse noted. "Companies should find ways to lower turnover if it takes this kind of toll on the bottom line."

"That's right," Sawyer agreed. "Unfortunately, many companies don't think about the loss of a better employee in terms of dollars and cents."

Jesse rubbed his thick brown hair and adjusted his glasses. "So you don't think that pay has that much to do with employees staying?"

"No, pay doesn't make them stay" answered Sawyer. "Unless of course the compensation package offered isn't competitive. In that case better employees will certainly leave."

"Will it get harder to attract quality employees in the future?" Jesse probed.

"Absolutely," Sawyer confirmed, "the bottom line is that people are retiring and more jobs are being created than we have qualified people to fill them. That trend will continue for at least ten years."

Jesse shook his head. "How will companies fare if they don't have a strategy for keeping better employees?"

"They'll be left behind," answered Sawyer. Sawyer leaned back and removed his resting elbows from the mahogany desk and said, "We have no intention for you to be one of those companies.

"You're still ready to become a People Keeper aren't you?" Sawyer chuckled half-jokingly as he led Jesse down the award-decorated hallway.

"Even more so," said Jesse as he followed close behind.

Two doors down from his own office, Sawyer stopped and reached in his pocket. After fumbling for the key, he opened the door and motioned for his friend to enter.

Jesse glanced at Sawyer and then stepped inside. The shiny gold name plate on the desk instantly captured his attention:

Jesse Shands
The People Keeper

"What's this?" Jesse asked.

"Your office, of course," Sawyer said, pleased with Jesse's enthusiasm. "It's yours to use this week as you learn how to become a People Keeper. The People Keeper consists of Five Tenets, they are on your desk. I've asked each of my managers to make themselves available whenever you want to visit with them. Now, I'm going fishing for the next two days, but I'll return on Friday so we can meet before you leave."

With that, Sawyer turned to Jesse and did something that surprised him. He prayed for God to bless Jesse's efforts to become a People Keeper.

Jesse sat down at the desk and began reading from the leather journal that contained the Five Tenets of the People Keeper.

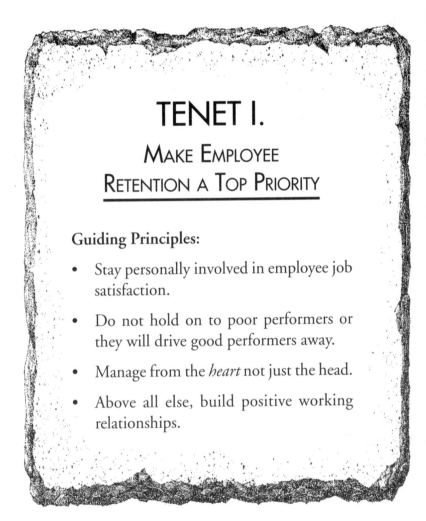

TENET I.

MAKE EMPLOYEE RETENTION A TOP PRIORITY

Guiding Principles:

- Stay personally involved in employee job satisfaction.

- Do not hold on to poor performers or they will drive good performers away.

- Manage from the *heart* not just the head.

- Above all else, build positive working relationships.

CHAPTER FOUR

The First Tenet

Make Employee Retention a Top Priority

Reading the First Tenet produced several questions for Jesse. He looked down the list of managers that Sawyer had left on the desk and decided that Human Resources would be an excellent place to start. He dialed the extension.

After a quick conversation on the phone, Jean invited Jesse down to her office.

When he arrived at Jean's open door, a sharply dressed brunette in her late fifties stood to greet him.

"Hi Jesse, I'm Jean," she announced making her way over to shake hands. "So you want to become a People Keeper?" she smiled.

"I sure do," answered Jesse, as he sat down he noticed a brass-framed quote on her wall.

*Employees will work
for a good company
but they will leave
a lousy boss.*

"Seems kind of unusual for a Human Resources Manager to have that hanging on the wall," Jesse remarked.

"Not in a People Keeper company," Jean said. "You see, we've found that the job satisfaction of the employee mostly comes down to the manager."

"I'm a little surprised by that. I know from Sawyer that pay doesn't make employees stay, but I thought that the work climate, the challenge of the job and morale considerably influenced job satisfaction," Jesse explained.

"They do," Jean replied warmly, "but who mainly impacts those factors?"

"The manager does," admitted Jesse.

"That's why the manager must make employee retention a top priority," remarked Jean. "Otherwise, work climate, morale and the employee's performance suffer. Being a People Keeper is the surest way to succeed with employees."

Jesse looked at Jean attentively as she talked. He liked her genuine belief in the People Keeper. "How do you know whether a manager is making People Keeping a priority?" he asked.

"Results!" Jean replied. "The evidence is in the results that they produce with their people. We measure morale, productivity, quality of work and job satisfaction as indicators of a manager's effectiveness."

"How do you make the Five Tenets a part of your day, every day?" Jesse wanted to know.

"You want to know how to make the People Keeper a part of your daily work life," Jean said. She got up and turned the page on her flip chart situated in the corner of the roomy office.

"Here's an illustration we use in our People Keeper training that might help," Jean said. She handed Jesse a sheet of paper with a question printed at the top of the page:

What do managers do?

"Answer that question by making a list and then read it off when you're finished," Jean instructed.

Jesse made a list and read it aloud:

Supervise	Praise
Delegation	Scheduling
Planning	Solving Problems
Budgeting	Discipline
Instruction	Give Feedback
Training	

After Jesse finished, Jean complimented him. "That's a good list and it came out just the way 90 percent of the managers here first answer that question," she said.

Jesse glanced at her with quizzing eyes.

"Your list breaks down into two categories — things that managers do which come from the *head*, and those things which come from the *heart*," Jean explained. "Like most managers, you thought mostly about activities that come from the *head*. For example, to supervise, delegate, budget, schedule, solve problems and discipline all require *head* skills."

"What's wrong with the list being dominated by *head* functions?" asked Jesse.

"It's the opposite of what employees say they'd like to see in a leader," Jean said. "Head functions don't contribute greatly to developing positive relationships with employees — and that's essential to being a People Keeper. Now look at your list again, how many *heart* functions do you see?"

"Praise is the only one I listed," Jesse answered as he glanced at the list again. "I think I get where you're headed with all this."

"And where's that?" asked Jean, smiling.

"Most managers spend too little time on the heart side of managing. Employees' needs aren't met if their boss only leads with head-driven activities versus heart-driven ones. Also, I don't think that many employees significantly admire or respect a boss for their head skills. I can just hear an employee saying, 'That manager of mine can sure make out a budget,'" Jesse said laughing.

The two professionals indulged themselves in the humor of the moment. They both knew that laughter definitely had its place in the work climate.

"Why do you think the manager's list is so different from the employee's list?" she asked.

"Perspective," Jesse answered, "I think it would be helpful if more managers could see for themselves what kinds of things employees rate as significant, maybe then they'd devote themselves more consistently to the heart-driven issues."

"You think that managers need the employee's perspective on this before they'll be motivated to change," Jean stated. "Okay, let's look at the Top 10 list together," she retrieved a file from her desk and handed Jesse a copy.

WHAT EMPLOYEES SAY
THEY WANT IN A MANAGER
■■■■■■■■■■■■■■■■■■■■■■■■

Integrity	Trust
Caring	Appreciation or Praise
Respect	Fairness
Listening	Teamwork
Communication	Decisiveness

"Now I want to be very clear about this list," Jean continued. "We're not talking about de-emphasizing the head skills in a manager. Rather, we find that you best become a People Keeper by gaining competence at the head *and* the heart issues of managing.

"Think about it — what top performer would want to work for a nice boss with lousy managerial skills?" asked Jean.

"Right, I get your point," remarked Jesse. "I see clearly now that being equally effective at the head *and* the heart issues helps retain better people — and saves time in the long run. Time otherwise spent on replacing key employees, doing job interviews, orientations, training, coaching, etcetera. It occurs to me that being a People Keeper doesn't have to take a lot of time, but it costs more time if you aren't."

Jean was glad that Jesse had absorbed so much and was already thinking like a People Keeper.

"You have to wonder why a company would continue to invest in advertising, interviewing, and training if there was a better way," she said. "Which companies are spending too much on employee turnover? It's the companies that haven't made employee motivation and retention a priority. Just exactly what kind of reputation do you think those companies will have in their community as an employer?"

"A poor one," answered Jesse. "What I'm seeing is that each organization has a choice — they can become a *Last-*

Resort or a *First-Choice Employer.* The outcome is directly related to the priorities of that organization. And if they create a mediocre reputation as an employer, it will result in attracting a lower quality employee for the future."

"Definitely," said Jean. "Top performers want to work for an employer who appreciates and values their contribution. Let me give you an example that makes a point that I hope you take back to your company.

"A big, prestigious manufacturer lost over one hundred production workers and managers to a chicken processing plant across the street. Why did those employees leave for similar pay but a far less glamorous job? Simple, the chicken processing plant is a First-Choice Employer — managed by People Keepers."

"How do you know that?" interrupted Jesse, a little surprised.

"Because the plant was once owned by Sawyer," Jean answered, "and his People Keepers stayed on to run things when he sold the business. The point I want to make is that anyone can become a First-Choice Employer even when the job or the pay isn't an advantage. Personally, I'm baffled as to why so few companies try to differentiate themselves from the status quo — and do so little to protect their better employees' job satisfaction."

"I don't know either," responded Jesse. "Maybe organizations just haven't devoted as much effort to differentiating themselves to employees like they have for customers. Stand out, offer something unique, be better, faster, and offer greater value for your customer — most organizations are quick to do that. By comparison, few invest enough in becoming First-Choice Employers."

Again, Jean was struck by Jesse's clear reasoning. She could see why Sawyer thought so much of him.

"But I'm struggling with an issue in my company that I need some advice on," Jesse continued. "I know that the People Keeper is about keeping good performers, but how does a People Keeper handle poor performers?"

Jean thought for a moment. "Let me ask you this question first — why is it critical to act *quickly* when you have a poor performer?"

"Because a poor performer will drive good performers away or drag everyone down to their level," Jesse said. "What company can afford either of those outcomes?"

Jean nodded. "Timeliness is key when dealing with poor performers," she said. "The biggest mistake employers make when dealing with a poor performer is to hold on too long, trying to convert that poor performer into a star. Nearly half of all employees in one survey I've read indicated that managers tolerate poor performers too long."

"Are you saying that poor performers can't change or become productive team members again?" Jesse asked.

"No, but the possibility of that happening is slim," Jean said. "But *never* risk the work-life satisfaction of your better employees because you're afraid of losing a 'warm body.' It takes courage to terminate someone who won't turn around when you're short on people anyway."

"That's a great point," Jesse said. "But I don't think you got around to answering my question as to how a People Keeper deals with poor performers."

"Get that notebook of yours ready," Jean said smiling. "There are four intervention steps that a People Keeper uses with poor performers. First, stay close to the situation. You can do this by checking on the employee every day. Second, shorten the time cycles for performance appraisals, meeting weekly if necessary. Set clear goals and deadlines for improvement and then stick to them.

"Third, keep your good performers in the loop," continued Jean. "Talk with them and ask whether they think the employee will be salvageable. Determine if they really want that person on the team. If not, why would you want to keep them? Finally, talk with the employee's customers or cross-functional teammates. Ask how well their needs are being met by the employee. How likely is it that a quality employee would stay motivated to work for an employer who tolerates poor performers?"

"Very unlikely," Jesse said as he finished writing down the four steps. He realized that he could use her advice in his own company.

"So," Jean said, "a People Keeper is successful because they stay personally involved with an employee's job satisfaction, and they intervene with poor performers when necessary. Now, here's the secret to making the employee's job satisfaction a priority and seeing great results in your company — relate well with your people. Relating positively with your better employees is critical to motivation and retention.

"Come with me," and with that Jean stood up, ushered Jesse out the door to the main floor which was full of activity. "Look over there by that big red storage unit, what do you see going on between that manager, the one in the blue tie, and his employees?"

"They're talking and enjoying themselves," answered Jesse.

"Yes, and do you know why?" Jean asked.

"No."

"Let me point out two dynamics here. First, the manager makes it a priority to interact and to be accessible. Some managers spend time trying to distance themselves from their people. A People Keeper makes sure that they can be reached by phone, e-mail, voice mail, or an appointment if necessary for a one-on-one talk. What kind of communication can a manager possibly develop with an employee if they aren't reasonably accessible?

"Second, that manager isn't reluctant to get on his employees' level to listen and talk *with* them, not *at* them. Now look over there, just beyond that row of crates. Four guys sit at those drafting tables all day long and crank out the schematics that one of our divisions uses. Their People Keeper is dynamite, she's one of the best we have. Those four men in her area have the utmost respect for her."

"Why?" Jesse wanted to learn her secrets.

"Because she respects them," answered Jean. "When they have a concern, she listens to it carefully. She's approachable, unlike some managers who give off an air that you better tread lightly. She also takes time to get to know each of them by taking an appropriate interest in their life outside of work."

Jesse and Jean stayed and watched several other interactions between People Keepers and their employees. Jesse was struck by the upbeat attitude that was so prevalent. "The interactions between People Keepers and employees are more relaxed and positive," he thought to himself. "The discussions seem to leave employees feeling energized." He noticed something else, too — the managers appeared to spend more time *listening* than talking.

When the two returned to Jean's office she asked him to recap what he had just learned.

How To Relate With Employees

- Be accessible. Have e-mail, voice mail or be available by phone when you can't be there in person.

- Spend time interacting. Let employees get to know you, and be on their level. Talk *with* them not *at* them. Listen more.

- Take an interest in their life outside of work — and their welfare at work. Ask about family, hobbies, sporting events, etc.

- Be quick to praise and encourage. Notice when they get something almost right, don't wait until it's perfect before you compliment them.

- Leave employees feeling better and more energized than you found them.

"To be truthful, these principles seem awfully simple," Jesse pointed out.

"Yes, most of the really effective principles for dealing with people are," Jean agreed. "You'll find that the People Keeper method is purposely simple, and anyone can master the Five Tenets." Jean got up and began pacing behind her desk.

"The ancient wisdom of the tenets has an almost supernatural way of taking you to your fullest potential as a manager," she said. "It brings out the strengths that you already possess while directly confronting your shortcomings. The People Keeper represents a powerful way of living out your role as a manager of people. Sawyer has a saying I use a lot:

*The People Keeper is
a positive way of living
with the people who you
manage, versus managing
to live with people.*

"Look back at the list that you made on relating with employees and tell me what you think that you need to improve upon the most?" Jean probed.

Jesse instantly knew which one he would start working on first. "I need to listen better," he said. "But I'd also like to know how to leave my employees feeling uplifted and energized after I've talked with them."

"Have you read the Second Tenet yet?"

"No, who should I talk with about it?"

"Why don't you talk with some of our employees about the Second Tenet," Jean asked.

"Talk directly with your employees? You're okay with that?" Jesse questioned.

"Sure, I'll have the management team pull together a group of employees in the conference room," Jean said as she walked around the desk and gave him a reassuring squeeze on the shoulder. "You're going to be a great People Keeper, Jesse."

Jesse thanked Jean and left her office feeling quite firm in his commitment to become a People Keeper. He realized that change started with deciding to improve, *now.* "Improvement only comes after you admit that there's a problem," he thought. Openly admitting to others and to himself that his company had its challenges with employee turnover and morale was a lot easier now.

At that moment, Jesse decided to do something that would later prove significant in his rapid progress as the People Keeper. He wrote a contract to himself:

Contract With Myself

I recognize that employee retention must be a significant priority in my company. I commit today to improve at keeping good employees and getting the most from their abilities. I expect a profitable return on this investment, with lower turnover costs that save the company money and increase our competitiveness through a loyal, experienced employee base. I *will* become a great People Keeper. Every day I will renew this contract with myself.

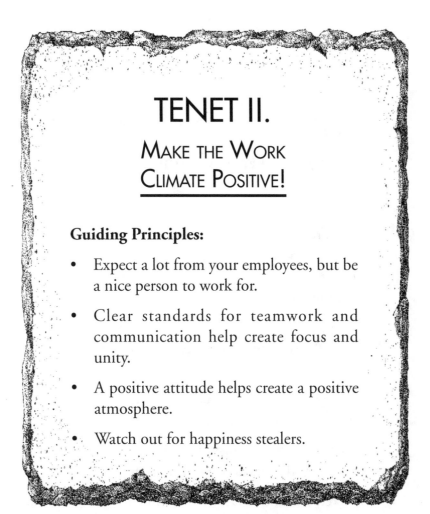

TENET II.

MAKE THE WORK CLIMATE POSITIVE!

Guiding Principles:

- Expect a lot from your employees, but be a nice person to work for.

- Clear standards for teamwork and communication help create focus and unity.

- A positive attitude helps create a positive atmosphere.

- Watch out for happiness stealers.

CHAPTER FIVE

The Second Tenet
Make the Work Climate Positive!

J esse entered the conference room and greeted five employees, who all seemed glad to see him. He thanked them for coming and said, "Working for Sawyer must be quite satisfying."

"Yes," said the chubby, balding man everyone called Davis, his last name. "Working for People Keepers makes all the difference."

"How do People Keepers make working here more satisfying than other places you've worked?" Jesse asked.

"They try real hard," answered Davis, he had put in 13 years working in the accounting department.

Jesse liked the enthusiasm he felt in this room. "What are some of the things that your managers do to make the work climate more positive?" he asked.

"I think one of the things that our managers do is that they try to be nice to work for," Carol said. She was an especially articulate woman with thick, appealing auburn hair who had worked as lead clerk in the shipping department for almost eight years.

"What do you mean by that?" Jesse asked.

"For one thing, they're easier to please," replied Carol.

"You mean they relax their standards?" Jesse questioned.

"No!" Carol shot back. "I didn't say easy to please, I said *easier*." Her fellow employees were nodding their heads, insisting in unison that the standards were not relaxed at all.

"Look," Davis added, "they never relax the standards here. In fact, they have very high expectations for all of us, but they aren't hard-to-please, slow-to-praise Neanderthals who run things with 'old school' management tactics. In fact, I think our managers are nicer to work for because they encourage us and they keep things positive."

"Yes, I agree," said Carol. "I also appreciate the fact that if I goof up my manager makes it a point to talk with me about the situation without threatening me or getting irate."

"Do you face much pressure on the job or is it pretty easy going?" Jesse probed. His question produced smirks on the faces of several employees. "What, did I strike a chord on something?" Jesse asked, smiling.

Robert, a 20-year veteran of the parts department, offered the answer. "Mr. Shands, the pressure here is intense, this is a very fast-paced environment and quality standards are quite high. But the difference is that our managers notice the times when we're under extreme pressure and they try to lighten things up."

"How do they do that?" asked Jesse.

"They might throw a pizza party or have sandwiches catered in," Davis said. "But mainly it's just in their attitude toward us. They seem to recognize when it's a high pressure time and they go out of their way not to add to it!"

"And the pizza parties and other extras definitely boost morale," Carol said.

The expression on Davis' face revealed that he wanted to say something. "I think another thing that positively impacts our working atmosphere is the open communication that we have," he said.

"What do you mean?" Jesse wanted to know.

"Well, my manager gets our team together weekly and we talk through the issues and the problems in the department," replied Davis. "That gets everything out in the open and it really helps to keep everything in perspective."

"And let me mention," Robert said, "that's one of the biggest differences you'll see in a People Keeper — they make it a priority to spend time with us."

Natalie, a slender young lady in her mid-twenties, worked in administrative support. She sat quietly until now. "The real difference to me is that the managers here treat employees as their equals," she said.

The other employees were a little stunned that Natalie, normally very shy, had spoken up. Robert encouraged her by showing his agreement with a nod, and she took his prodding positively, saying, "I get the feeling that the company and my boss considers *me* a valuable resource."

That struck Jesse positively. "How does your manager convey to you that you're an important member of the team here?" he asked.

"Well, he really respects us for one thing," Natalie said. "You can tell because when you talk with him, he carefully considers what you have to say."

"It's the only place I've ever worked where the managers come out of their office on a regular basis to communicate with employees in positive ways," added Sandy. She was a quiet but elegant woman that worked in marketing as a graphic designer.

All the employees nodded in agreement. "Can you see, Mr. Shands, how this company is different from the norm?" Carol asked. "Can you see now why we're proud to work for a First-Choice Employer?"

"I sure can," Jesse replied. "I've never seen a company like yours. I've been taking notes as fast as I can and here's what I have so far:

BEING A NICE PERSON TO WORK FOR

- Being a nice boss doesn't mean that you relax your standards.

- Notice when your employees are under a lot of pressure or stress, and then lighten things up. Add some humor, bring in pizza, etc.

- Maintain open communication because employees like regular dialogue and it helps create a more positive working relationship.

- Treat employees like a valuable, equal partner in the pursuit of your goals.

"I'll add my two cents to that," Natalie said, thrusting one finger in the air. "Teamwork is a big part of the reason I enjoy it here so much. And it's one of the reasons that I'm content staying here. I've worked for other companies where the employees and sometimes even the managers didn't co-operate or get along. I was miserable."

"Why do you think it's different at Sawyer's company?" asked Jesse.

"Because the managers make teamwork and communication a priority," answered Natalie.

"How many of you agree?" Jesse wanted to know. Every hand went up. "So what's the secret to better teamwork?" Jesse was anxious to learn.

"The 8 Standards of Teamwork and Communication," they all said.

"It's an easy-to-use tool that helps ensure that we focus on the standards which are important in working together to accomplish our goals," Carol explained.

"Who selects the 8 Standards?" asked Jesse.

"The team does," replied Carol. She got up, went to the corner of the room where two stacks of paper laid on a work table and brought a copy to Jesse. "Each department narrows this list down to the 8 standards that are most important to their teamwork and communication."

20 STANDARDS of TEAMWORK & COMMUNICATION

Not Important	Slightly Important	Average Importance	Very Important	Extremely Important
1	2	3	4	5

1 _____ **INTEGRITY/HONESTY** — We uphold the organization's values and business ethics.

2 _____ **COOPERATION** — We are team players, cooperating and helping each other. We put our team objectives ahead of personal agendas. People work well together to meet goals.

3 _____ **LISTENING SKILL** — We give undivided attention when others speak. We seek to understand, not just hear what others say.

4 _____ **OPEN COMMUNICATION** — We take the initiative to communicate regularly between our different teams. We keep each other well-informed.

5 _____ **PLANNING AND ORGANIZATION** — We plan out actions for the future in a proactive, organized manner. We lay out clear steps, alert proper individuals in advance, and establish deadlines.

6 _____ **DECISIVENESS** — We make decisions and take action in a timely manner.

7 _____ **PROBLEM SOLVING** — We identify and admit our problems, assess possible actions and reach quality solutions.

8 _____ **DIRECTION/GOALS** — We develop a clear picture of where the team or organization is headed and what is to be accomplished, and communicate it clearly to everyone who needs to know.

9 _____ **TRUST** — Our working relationship is built on trust. We believe and act on what our teammates say.

10 _____ **COMMITMENT** — We are committed to the mission, goals, and progress of the organization or team. We remain actively committed during times of opposition or challenge.

11 _____ **PRAISE/APPRECIATION** – We express our appreciation for each other's efforts and achievements. We give genuine praise and celebrate our accomplishments.

12 _____ **RESPECT/CONCERN FOR OTHERS** – We are considerate and treat each other with respect. We value our fellow employees and their contributions. We treat each other's opinions and ideas as importantly as our own.

13 _____ **POSITIVE WORK CLIMATE** – We work together to maintain an upbeat work climate and good attitudes.

14 _____ **OPEN AND APPROACHABLE** – We have an atmosphere of openness to new ideas. We get our problems or concerns with each other out in the open in healthy ways.

15 _____ **CLEAR EXPECTATIONS** – We make sure that our expectations and needs are clear when we work collaboratively between teams or departments.

16 _____ **COMMITTED TO QUALITY** – We strive to get the job done right the first time. We are committed both to quality and continuous improvement.

17 _____ **SOMEBODY/NOBODY/EVERYBODY** – If Somebody drops the ball and Nobody picks it up, Everybody loses. We pick up dropped balls for one another, i.e. mistakes, oversights and blunders.

18 _____ **PROACTIVE** – We take initiative, within the empowerment given, to implement best business practices, pursue new ideas, and take calculated risks to achieve goals.

19 _____ **CUSTOMER** – We are committed to delivering exceptional value to our customers. We give customers outstanding, timely service. We dedicate ourselves to finding ways to further increase customer satisfaction.

20 _____ **CHANGE** – We adapt to and/or foster change in order to best capitalize on opportunity.

Jesse read it and said, "Don't misunderstand what I'm about to say, because I see this tool being extremely helpful. But I could apply it better if I knew why having a set of clear standards is so important."

"Let me ask you a question," Robert said. "If a team doesn't have a clear set of standards for how they will work and communicate together, and let's say that there are ten people on the team, how many different sets of standards do you potentially have?"

"Ten," answered Jesse. "But what's the significance of having *specific standards*? Don't people already know how they're supposed to work and communicate together?"

"Not so," Carol answered. "Most people have different opinions about what's important. Many never really think about what should guide their attitude or actions, they just fall in line with the pack. Sawyer has a saying around here that makes the point well."

In the absence of clear standards people create their own.

Jesse wrote that down and he saw what the employees were getting at. "What people want are clear standards because it shows them what's expected and it creates continuity in how things should be done. Standards help build stronger teamwork and performance!"

"You've nailed it!" exclaimed Carol and Sandy together, smiling.

"Now do you see how standards contribute to a more positive work climate?" Sandy asked.

"I sure do," replied Jesse. "It's obvious to me now that clear standards remove ambiguity and put the focus on what's most important. Standards improve the likelihood that employees will perform more consistently and accomplish their goals. Now what I need to know is how to better use this tool, now that I understand why it works."

"Okay, maybe this picture will help," Robert replied. He passed a single page from his notebook to Jesse.

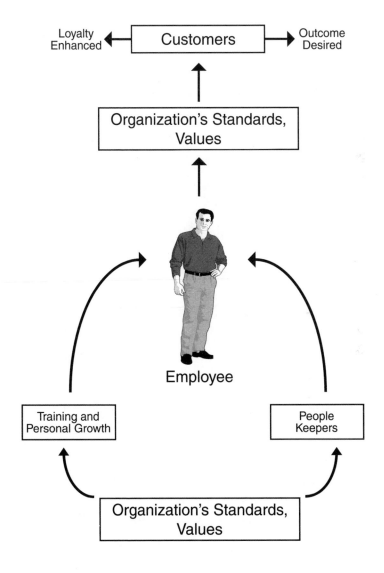

"What's the first thing that strikes you about this picture?" asked Robert.

Jesse looked it over and said, "That the customer is at the top where they belong."

"Excellent," Robert said. "That's what we believe too. Our standards should ultimately impact the customer in a way that we get the desired outcome — enhanced loyalty."

"I get it," Jesse said with enthusiasm, "the organization's standards and values should guide the attitudes and actions of its employees, so that it brings about the experience that you want the customer to have."

"Absolutely," Sandy affirmed.

"Now if I'm understanding this right, the employees are impacted by the standards through their People Keepers and through training."

"That's right," Carol said. "Do you know why People Keepers and training are so important to positively impacting employees and getting the correct outcome?"

"I think I do," answered Jesse. "For employees to take standards seriously, it's imperative that People Keepers believe in and model those standards themselves."

"Correct," Davis confirmed. "If you don't model the standards, you can bet that your employees will take them for granted."

"When it comes to training and personal growth, what our managers do is pretty smart," said Robert. "Instead of just a one time immersion in this stuff, they continually reinforce it, kind of like being sprinkled every day instead of dunked just once. The way that managers emphasize the 8 Standards is they discuss them in monthly meetings and at employee training and coaching sessions. They also make it a point to praise us for practicing the standards."

"Wow, that is smart," noted Jesse under his breath.

"It's impossible to work here and not know what the 8 Standards are," Natalie said. "You get indoctrinated the day you start, and it *never* stops. I think if our managers didn't regularly emphasize the 8 Standards and hold us accountable for them, eventually it would lose its significance."

Robert, Davis, Carol, and Sandy all acknowledged their agreement.

"People Keeping isn't a program, it's a way of living and leading others," Sandy remarked. "That's why we never want to quit working with each other on our teamwork and communication standards."

Jesse realized that teamwork and communication standards would create the kind of working atmosphere that his company needed. He sighed deeply and looked down at the picture again.

"What's wrong?" Sandy asked.

"Oh, I just realized that I have 51 sets of standards running my company and I've really overlooked something essential," Jesse admitted.

"Better late than never," Natalie said, smiling warmly. "Put that thought in your rearview mirror and move forward, focusing on what you can do about changing the atmosphere in your company."

The group nodded, they couldn't agree more. They knew that People Keepers didn't spend time regretting past mistakes, instead they made things a little better today, every day.

"Mr. Shands, Sawyer has a saying around here that may help," Natalie offered.

Improve 1 percent a day and in 70 days you'll be 100 percent better."

"That's great," Jesse said, writing it down. "You know, it would be beneficial to me if you could walk me through one of your 8 Standards of Teamwork and Communication and explain why it works so well," Jesse remarked.

"I'd love to," Sandy said. "Here's my personal favorite."

Somebody
Nobody
Everybody

Robert abruptly shot up from his chair, walked over to the corner of the room and picked up a football. He turned around and tossed it to Jesse, who caught it with pen still in hand.

"Good catch," joked Robert.

"What this means," Sandy said ignoring the guy-thing going on in the room, "is that if *Somebody* on our team drops the ball, and *Nobody* picks it up, then *Everybody* loses. But if *Somebody* will pick up the ball, *Everybody* can win. This standard says that we will help our teammates whenever something has been overlooked, or a mistake has been made."

"For example, if someone messes up on a customer's order you step in and correct it even if it's not your mistake," Carol said. "You can deal with why it happened later, for now you take care of the customer."

"It's my favorite standard too, because I like the football," Davis said, hoping to get the guy-thing going again.

Jesse looked down and noticed that the football had *Somebody, Nobody, Everybody* printed in big black letters just under the threads. "I like this illustration–and I'm going to use it with my team," he said as he faked a pass to Davis.

"In all seriousness," remarked Davis, "the football is a clever way of getting you to see the bigger picture of teamwork—that we're all on the same team regardless of position or department. It's a constant reminder that you need others on your team to be a winner."

Jesse gave the football a soft toss to Natalie and asked, "What makes you so willing to pick up a ball you didn't drop?"

"Because I know that you'd do it for me if the roles were reversed," Natalie answered without pause. "Anyone who works here better help others or they won't make it very long."

"They'd be fired?" Jesse wondered.

"Probably not," Sandy answered, "they'd probably be weeded out on their own. Non-team players stand out like a sore thumb–and they know it. Most leave before the manager ever has to intervene."

"The other reason that I'd pick up the ball is because I don't want to do anything that might undermine our terrific work climate," Natalie added. "In fact, I've never understood why so many companies do so little to keep their employee's morale high.

"From what Sawyer says, most companies spend around 40 percent of their budget on wages and benefits and less than one percent on things that maintain morale," Natalie said.

"With good employees so hard to come by, you have to wonder why more companies don't invest in keeping good employees happy and productive," Jesse pondered. "What would you say is the most important key to creating a positive work climate?"

"The manager's attitude!" the five employees said together.

"Why do you feel so strongly about that?" Jesse asked.

"Because a positive work climate starts with a positive attitude from the manager," Carol said. "How likely is it that you could have a positive work climate where there's a manager with a crummy attitude?"

"Carol's right," Davis added as everyone agreed. "Everyone who works here has probably heard this Sawyer saying I'm about to give you:

The characteristics of the king will be seen in the kingdom.

"So, a People Keeper's attitude, whether it's positive or crummy, will influence the behavior of employees," Jesse stated.

"Exactly," responded Davis, "managers are as positive or negative as they choose to be. The best People Keepers choose to be positive every day. Let me give you an illustration that I've heard Sawyer use before.

"Let's suppose that we put one negative person in a room with one positive person," Davis continued. "Researchers actually find that after 10 minutes, the negative person will have the positive person primarily talking and thinking about negative things. And if you put two positive persons in the room with him it will take twenty minutes, but the negativist will have the two positive people mainly thinking and talking about negative things. Finally, it will take three positive people to outweigh the negativist so that the positive individuals can still think and talk about some things that are positive. Now why do you think the negativist has such a strong influence on others?"

"Because it's quicker and easier to tear down than it is to build up," Jesse answered.

"Right," Davis said. "How devastating is the impact of a negativist?"

"Incredibly devastating," replied Jesse. "I get what you're saying now. How long would a person want to be around a leader who tears down rather than builds up?"

"Correct," said Carol. "Who wants to work at a company like that, with a boss like that? Sawyer once told me, 'A positive attitude can't be taught it must be caught.'"

"But some people never 'catch' it," Jesse pointed out. "No matter how much effort you invest in turning their attitude around, they never change."

"That's right, and we call those people happiness stealers, because they don't just harm themselves," Robert said. "They also rob others of joy and satisfaction."

"So what do your managers do about happiness stealers?" asked Jesse.

"Cut them off," Davis answered. "Our managers go to a negative employee and let them know that their attitude is hindering the team. They set a deadline for improvement and then stick to it."

"In other words, if they don't shape up, the manager ships them out," said Natalie.

This didn't surprise Jesse. He was learning that in order to be a First-Choice Employer and attract quality employees, you had to trim undesirable employees from the team.

"If you want to be a People Keeper you better not allow negative employees to steal the happiness of your better employees," Sandy said.

"Negativity is not only toxic, it's infectious," Carol explained. "It can start with just a few people but quickly spread to other departments and then to the whole company, weakening the organization's ability to accomplish goals."

"Keep your work climate positive or you may lose your very best employees," Robert said. "It's that simple."

"That's a great point to end on," said Jesse. He stood and thanked the employees for their help. "You guys have helped make the Second Tenet so clear that I now see several practical steps I can take to create a more positive work climate."

Jesse smiled and raised his hand in farewell to the employees. Sawyer was truly blessed to have attracted and retained such quality people. He quickly scanned his thorough notes, and with no time to waste, Jesse hustled back to the office and opened the leather journal to the Third Tenet.

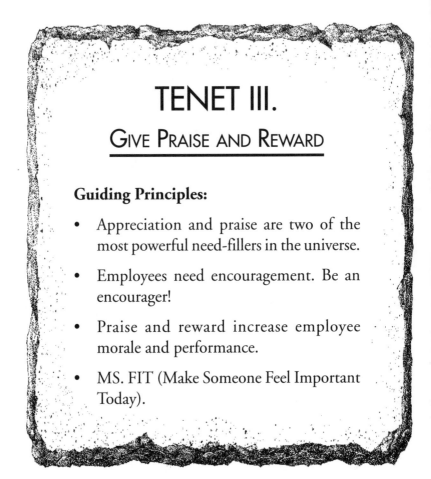

TENET III.

GIVE PRAISE AND REWARD

Guiding Principles:

- Appreciation and praise are two of the most powerful need-fillers in the universe.

- Employees need encouragement. Be an encourager!

- Praise and reward increase employee morale and performance.

- MS. FIT (Make Someone Feel Important Today).

CHAPTER SIX

The Third Tenet
Give Praise and Reward

Jesse stood up from the desk after reading the Third Tenet and looked out the spacious window. The temporary office that Sawyer provided was a good place to reflect.

He realized that praise and reward were not among his strengths. "Have my employees noticed my lack of praise and encouragement?" he wondered. He had falsely assumed that good performers already knew that they performed well and therefore didn't need to be told.

Gazing out the window at the tall oak trees that shielded the office from the intense winter sun, Jesse had an idea. He left the office and roamed throughout the company asking employees and managers who they considered to be great at the Third Tenet. If he was going learn, he wanted to learn from the best.

One name surfaced repeatedly, Rudy, an assistant supervisor for the warehouse. Jesse knocked on Rudy's office door and was instantly greeted by an energetic, "Come on in."

Rudy, a very thin man in his mid to late fifties, had deep set blue eyes but a big friendly smile that lit up the room. Jesse noticed that Rudy was wheelchair bound and that his body pitched slightly to the left. Bearing the obvious signs of some cruelly disabling disease, he was a surprisingly cheerful gentleman.

Jesse reached across the desk as the two men shook hands. Rudy said, "I've heard a lot of good things about you."

"Thank you," Jesse responded. It amazed him that communication traveled so quickly throughout Sawyer's company. "I'm here to learn how to become a People Keeper."

"Wonderful, so what brought you to see me?" Rudy asked.

"The Third Tenet," Jesse responded. "A number of managers and employees suggested that I talk with you. They feel that you're a great example of how to praise others."

Rudy smiled back and said with a great deal of humility, "That's awfully kind of them to say that, but I'm not deserving. I'd love to help you any way that I can."

"One way you can help is to explain why the Third Tenet is important to being a People Keeper," Jesse probed.

"So you want to know why praise is so important to being an effective People Keeper," remarked Rudy with pleasure. "That's a good place to start. The best way to answer that question is to ask another question first — why do employees need praise?"

"Sure," replied Jesse. "I think praise makes employees feel better about themselves and I think it serves as a motivator."

"That shows insight, but now let me show you some other reasons that I think explain clearly why praise is so vital," Rudy said.

Jesse took the laminated reminder tool from Rudy's extended hand and looked it over carefully:

WHY EMPLOYEES NEED PRAISE
■■■■■■■■■■■■■■■■■■■■■■■■■

- Praise encourages employees and makes them feel appreciated.

- Praise builds confidence and makes employees feel important. Everyone wants and needs to feel competent and capable, and praise helps meet that need.

- Praise reinforces the behaviors that you consider most critical to your operations. Consequently, employees are more focused on accomplishing your priorities and goals.

- Praise raises performance levels.

"Since praise meets such deep, real needs in people, why would a manager wait until an annual performance review to give someone a little praise or encouragement?" Rudy asked.

"That would be like playing a year-long football game before you get to know the score!" Jesse remarked.

"Good analogy," complimented Rudy. "Isn't it frustrating when you feel that you've done a good job but it has gone unnoticed?"

"Yes," answered Jesse. Then he realized that he had been a manager just like that. He was slow to praise, quick to point out what wasn't done right. He didn't like that realization, but he was determined to change with Rudy's help.

"Jesse, do you like little sayings?" Rudy wondered as he turned in his wheelchair and pointed to a framed quote placed atop his book case.

MS. FIT
Make Someone Feel
Important Today!

"That's catchy and easy to remember," Jesse commented. "So a People Keeper praises and rewards people every day?"

"Only if the situation merits, maybe several times a day or just once in a week," Rudy said.

"Making someone feel important is important to making someone want to stay, isn't it?" asked Jesse.

"Precisely," answered Rudy. "When a People Keeper makes a valued employee feel important, that employee will stay motivated and will be more likely to stay."

"I see now why you're so good at praise Rudy," Jesse declared. "You really *want* employees to know that you appreciate and value them."

"You're right, praise comes from the heart, not just the head," Rudy responded.

"I hate to tell you this, but before I came here it was my belief that an employee knows when they've done a good job without me needing to tell them," Jesse admitted.

"Who sold you that lie?" Rudy demanded, almost coming out of his wheelchair for a moment. "Why would any manager want to hold something back that does so much good?"

"Well, I see that now," said Jesse. "But, a lot of managers have that attitude about praise."

"Are you familiar with the ancient proverb that goes something like *'Do not withhold good from those who deserve it when it is in your power to give it'*? Rudy asked.

Jesse shook his head that he was not.

"Well, I like that proverb because it reminds me to not be stingy, but rather to be generous with my praise. Believing that employees don't need to know that they're doing a fine job shows a lack of understanding about what employees need from their managers," cautioned Rudy. "If you want to become a great People Keeper and motivator you must not withhold praise from those that deserve it and you must learn to be an encourager."

"But what if it doesn't come naturally?" Jesse questioned.

"That's okay," Rudy answered. "It doesn't come naturally for ninety out of a hundred managers." Rudy gave Jesse a reassuring look and smile. "If you want, I'll give you an illustration and a reminder tool so you can see how simple it is to become an encourager."

"I'd really appreciate that," said Jesse.

"Let's start by supposing that you were asked to list people in your life who you consider to have been good encouragers. They could be parents, friends, teachers, children or whomever. Take a sheet of paper and make a list of two or three of those people right now." Rudy waited until Jesse had finished his list.

"Now, who's on your list?" asked Rudy.

Jesse mentioned his wife, a high school coach, and his mother.

"Great," Rudy said. "What if we could bring those people into this room, as well as some other people who know you well like your children, employees, acquaintances from church or a business club. And what if we asked them the same question — who in their life had been a good encourager to them?"

"Okay," Jesse said, still listening carefully.

"Now here's the question that Sawyer asked me when I did this with him, and I'll ask it of you — would *you* make *their* list?" Rudy asked.

"I doubt it," answered Jesse quietly. "I hope that I would, but, ..."

"We all hope that we would make that kind of impact on people we care about," responded Rudy more softly. "Who controls whether we make the list?"

"We do of course," Jesse said. "Anyone can be a good encourager, anyone can make the list, that's what you're saying, isn't it?"

"Exactly," said Rudy. "Being a good encourager begins with wanting to encourage people who you care about. Let me ask you this, why did you pick your mom as an encourager in your life?"

"Because my dad's death devastated me, I was only nine," answered Jesse. "Mom was always in my corner encouraging me. She said over and over that God had a great plan for my life and would use me in a big way some day, and I believed her."

"Isn't it amazing how far-reaching encouraging words can be?" Rudy asked.

"They last a lifetime," Jesse pointed out. "I see now that my words of encouragement can make a lasting memory for an employee, a friend, my children and my wife. I just have to want to and then take action."

"Right," remarked Rudy. "Now just add to that willingness of yours some practical principles and you'll be a great encourager." Rudy handed a reminder tool to Jesse:

HOW TO BE AN ENCOURAGER

- Be quick to build up and affirm employees. Everyone needs encouragement from time to time.

- Look for and act upon all opportunities to congratulate employees on a job well done. Don't fall into the trap of thinking it but not saying it.

- Focus more of your communication on the employee's capabilities than on their shortcomings. Reason: It's easy to notice someone's mistakes to the point that you no longer see their strengths.

- When an employee fouls up, encourage them. Try saying: *"I know you can improve on this, maybe there are some ways I can help you."*

"What key principle do you see in this reminder tool?" Rudy probed.

"I think I see what you're trying to get managers to do," stated Jesse. "You want People Keepers to see the positive side, and the good things that their employees do. You're trying to get managers to break out of the habit of seeing the downside all the time, aren't you?"

Rudy nodded. "How effective will you be as a motivator and People Keeper if your antenna is tuned into mostly negative stations?"

"And what kind of encourager will you be if you focus on the mistakes most of the time?" Jesse added. "Who'd want to work for a manager like that? I need a praise and reward program in my company."

"No, you don't," Rudy responded with some added emphasis as he fixed his eyes on Jesse's. "Look, praise and reward is an *attitude* that you have toward people, it's not a program that comes and goes. Don't make the two mistakes that so many companies make with praise and reward."

"What are they?" asked Jesse, still startled by Rudy's somewhat pointed response.

"First, doing it because everyone else is," answered Rudy. "Take the 'Employee of The Month Award' — most companies have them but few really work, which leads me to the second mistake. That's failing to think a reward or incentive-based recognition through in a way that it has clear goals and fits into your overall People Keeping strategy."

"I think I need an example to make this clear to me," Jesse remarked.

"Then I have the perfect blunder to tell you about," Rudy said.

"Last year a manager from a large retailer came here to learn how to become a People Keeper. We gladly shared everything she wanted to know but it was apparent to me that she wanted to take practices not principles with her. Her questions always focused on what we were doing and how we did it but hardly ever on *why* we rewarded and recognized. She wanted all the reminder tools and tips, but barely paid attention when we tried to explain the reasons behind them. Now let me tell you what she did when she returned to her company.

"Her idea was to start a rewards program that recognized the one employee each month that produced the highest cross-over sales. The winner would get to draw for a prize such as nice merchandise, an all-expense paid trip, or cash. That excited one young man so much that he decided to really go for it. He worked especially hard, followed up on each lead and even put in extra time. Even his wife was excited when his efforts paid off and he won the opportunity to draw for a prize.

"The manager gathered everyone around, placed a basket with plastic eggs in front of him and wished him luck. He picked an egg, opened it, and three jelly beans fell out. The young man looked up and thought it must be a joke, but no one was laughing. His manager took the basket and said 'better luck next time,'" Rudy said.

"That was a stupid thing to do," Jesse said sadly.

"I agree," Rudy stated. "It would have been better for that manager if she'd never started a rewards program. She demoralized the team and lost a good performer over it — in fact, he eventually came to work for us."

"Who can blame the young man for leaving a boss like that?" Jesse said. "So do you have any suggestions for knowing when to use praise and reward? You don't want to praise for anything and everything do you?"

"Of course not," answered Rudy. "What would be the point of that? That would make praise or reward so commonplace that they lose their value. Here are some situations that might merit praise or reward."

Jesse looked over the list of ideas that Rudy gave him.

WHEN TO USE PRAISE OR REWARD
■■■■■■■■■■■■■■■■■■■■■■■■■■■■■■■

- When the employee has done an exceptional job on a project or task.

- When the employee meets a deadline.

- When you receive a customer compliment.

- When an employee fulfills one of your cultural beliefs or values.

- When goals are achieved.

- When an employee goes the extra mile to help another team member.

- When an employee improves something in your operation.

- When people put in extra effort during busy times or for big deadlines.

- When they achieve consistency in quality, efficiency, results, etc.

- When an employee learns to do something new on their own.

- For speaking up honestly, or for giving ideas.

Jesse finished reading the list and he marked a few that caught his eye. As he read the list, a particular employee occasionally came to mind. He got excited about the possibilities of praise and rewards for employees. "What kinds of rewards do you give?" he asked.

"First of all, I'd like you to notice that some of the situations on this reminder tool are better served by praise while others deserve a reward," responded Rudy. "Do you know the difference?"

"Not really," admitted Jesse.

"One difference is that a reward should include specific criteria, while praise may or may not be based upon definite criteria," Rudy explained. "Praise is often given spontaneously when you catch something noteworthy happening. Rewards, on the other hand, are often given at regular intervals. Generally, rewards are given for specific, measurable achievements, i.e. a goal met, years of service, etcetera. A successful rewards effort should be based on a budget, whereas praise requires no budget. Would you like some ideas for giving rewards too?" asked Rudy.

"I'd love that," Jesse replied. "Thanks."

Rudy was already handing the reminder tool to Jesse.

Reward Ideas
■ ■ ■ ■ ■ ■ ■ ■ ■ ■ ■ ■

- Buy a baseball bat and engrave the rewarded employee's name on it. *Example*: For A Home Run Job!

- Erect a *Braggin' Board* for special employee accomplishments.

- Buy something for the employee's family or child like a cookie tray, or a toy. Leave a note such as: *Thanks for letting your dad work here.*

- Present a *Behind The Scenes Award* for someone whose efforts normally go unnoticed or unappreciated by others.

- Award a *Teamwork Trophy* for teams or work groups that have worked well together on a tough project.

- Buy a restaurant certificate, movie tickets or other items that the rewarded employee will enjoy.

- Have an upper executive or owner thank or praise the employee for their outstanding work. A written note would be a splendid memory maker.

- Award a company shirt or hat for an employee who achieved a goal.

- Ask the employee for a list of rewards they'd like that cost less than $25. When you catch them doing something rewardable, buy an item from their list.

- Award a certificate that allows them to come into work late or leave work early. Give it along with a gift certificate to a restaurant or coffee shop.

"Not everyone is motivated by the same rewards," Rudy said. "That's why I like to ask my employees for a list of things under $25, then I know what to buy them."

"That takes a little planning and time," observed Jesse.

"Of course, but it's well worth the look on their face and the warm fuzzies in their heart!" replied Rudy.

"Your employees must feel great when they get rewards like these," Jesse remarked as he scanned the list again. "And most of these don't cost very much at all, it's really the thought that counts."

"That's right," Rudy said. "The fact that we think enough of them to reward their efforts speaks volumes about our appreciation of their contributions."

"I can see why your company is so good at making employees feel important," said Jesse. "You've made it a part of your culture to treat employees that way."

"What do you mean?" Rudy was curious to know.

"You use praise and reward as the primary way of relating with employees," Jesse answered. "It's more than just an occasional thing around here, it's a definite priority for a People Keeper. No wonder your employees feel appreciated and want to stay working here. I want to know how to implement these ideas in a manner that will really work in my company."

"That's easier than you might think," Rudy said. "Around here, we use this reminder tool developed by Sawyer:

Be Consistent With
Praise and Reward
■ ■ ■ ■ ■ ■ ■ ■ ■ ■ ■ ■ ■ ■ ■ ■

- Don't wait until the employee gets it perfect. Acknowledge smaller steps of progress along the way.

- Make a list of what you appreciate about each employee. Review the list periodically and see if you've expressed any of these thoughts in awhile.

- Get in the habit of writing notes of appreciation or encouragement to employees. Set aside time to get this done and write it in on your schedule each month.

- When you see or hear something worth praising, mention it then before you forget it.

- Don't fall into the trap of letting your appreciation stockpile until the employee's annual performance appraisal. Praise and reward are most appreciated when it occurs throughout the year.

While Jesse read the reminder tool, he could see Rudy drawing something. Suddenly Rudy turned the paper around and asked, "What do you see?"

"Two red dots," Jesse answered. On the sheet of paper, Rudy had drawn two one-inch diameter circles and colored them red.

"Right," Rudy said. "But suppose we said that the white space represented all the good things about an employee's performance, their strengths, contributions, dependability, and so forth. And the two red dots represented all the mistakes, shortcomings and weaknesses of the employee. Which do you think most managers have a tendency by habit to see first?"

"The mistakes, of course" said Jesse.

"Why?" Rudy asked.

"Because we have a tendency as managers to more quickly and easily see the mistakes and foibles of others," Jesse replied. "It's human nature."

"You're right," confirmed Rudy. "After I'd worked in this job for three months, Sawyer came by my office one day. He did this exercise with me and asked me point blank — 'Rudy are you a red-dot manager?'"

"Was that embarrassing?" asked Jesse.

"Of course," Rudy said. "But only because it was true. I'm glad he did it, though, because it really opened my eyes to the fact that my red-dot management style was limiting what my people would accomplish. And it would limit what I would achieve as a manager and People Keeper. I know now that people perform better and stay longer with praise."

"You've made me a believer," Jesse said. "I can't tell you how much you've helped me understand this powerful principle, and you've given me some great reminder tools to get me started."

"Then you should be ready for the Fourth Tenet now," Rudy said, pleased that he had helped Jesse.

He handed a copy of the Fourth Tenet to Jesse and read it aloud, emphasizing certain words:

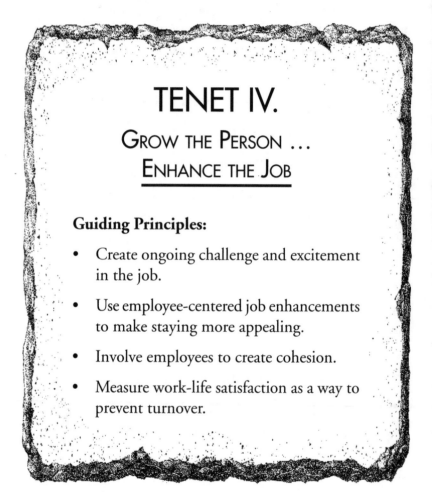

TENET IV.

GROW THE PERSON ...
ENHANCE THE JOB

Guiding Principles:

- Create ongoing challenge and excitement in the job.

- Use employee-centered job enhancements to make staying more appealing.

- Involve employees to create cohesion.

- Measure work-life satisfaction as a way to prevent turnover.

CHAPTER SEVEN

The Fourth Tenet
Grow the Person...Enhance the Job

When Rudy finished, he looked up at Jesse and said, "I have someone in mind that would be great to visit with you about the Fourth Tenet. Her name is Cynthia Hardy and she's the best at it in my mind."

"Great," Jesse said. "I'm excited to learn these principles because they seem especially important."

"You're right, they are," remarked Rudy as he dialed Cynthia's extension. "By the way, you'd better wear steel-toed shoes if you have a pair!"

Jesse smiled, not at all sure what Rudy meant. He shook Rudy's hand and headed to the training room where he was to meet Cynthia.

Jesse let himself in. As she concluded the training program she was presenting, Cynthia walked to the back of the room and said, "You must be Jesse Shands. I'm Cynthia."

"I'm here learning how to be a People Keeper, and Rudy tells me that you're the best at the Fourth Tenet," Jesse said as he took the nearest seat.

"Thank you, that's very kind of Rudy," Cynthia said. "I guess we all have our strengths as People Keepers. I'm just glad he didn't cover my weaknesses."

Jesse smiled and asked, "What is your greatest strength?"

"Getting the most out of a person," Cynthia said.

"Isn't that sort of contrary to the idea of being a People Keeper?" Jesse questioned.

"Not at all," answered Cynthia. "If a manager gets anything less than the most a person is capable of, then they haven't done a very effective job of growing that person. As a People Keeper, you want to view employees as valuable resources who have bountiful creativity, unlimited passion, and unseen potential, and it's your job to nurture it correctly."

"But I thought top performers were self-motivated, that you could put them on auto-pilot and get out of their way," said Jesse.

"Then you don't really know high performers very well," stated Cynthia with her famous candor. "I don't mean to be so direct, but you need to realize that keeping top performers satisfied requires periodic intervention by the manager."

"How exactly do you intervene?" Jesse inquired.

"That's a good question," remarked Cynthia. "The key is to have regular dialogue with your employee."

"Why is that so important to a People Keeper?" questioned Jesse.

"Let me demonstrate something that I think will help answer your question clearly," Cynthia stated confidently. "Pick a number between one and 100."

"Okay," Jesse said, willing to go along, "23."

"Not even close, it was 88," Cynthia said. "Suppose that I told you that you can ask me questions about my number before guessing, to narrow it down. Would your chances of getting the right number improve?"

"Of course," responded Jesse, not knowing where this was going.

"That's the point, isn't it — to know what an employee is thinking and feeling before they start looking around. When you keep regular dialogue and ask questions you get to know what they're thinking. Suppose an employee gets bored or frustrated with a job for some reason. We can intervene and develop a plan with the employee's help to make the work more challenging or rewarding. Then we have a chance to fix it before they are tempted to look elsewhere for work."

"Do you ever find that just getting the employee to talk about it clears a lot of it up?" asked Jesse.

"Yes, more often than you might think," Cynthia answered. "What does that tell you?"

"That employees want and need the opportunity to dialogue with their bosses," replied Jesse.

"Absolutely," confirmed Cynthia. "If a manager doesn't talk regularly with an employee, how can he expect to know that a good employee is getting discouraged? How will he know when to intervene?"

"Yeah," Jesse agreed. "How effective can they really be at keeping good employees from leaving if they're uninvolved?"

"They certainly aren't going to know how to best enrich the employee's job if they aren't communicating very often," Cynthia said.

"I was going to ask about that," said Jesse. "Do you have some ideas on how to enhance a job so that better employees want to stay?"

"Sure," replied Cynthia. "Here are some of the ways we've been doing it here." She handed Jesse the reminder tool:

Ways To Enhance Jobs
■■■■■■■■■■■■■■■■■■■■■■

- Give the employee autonomy to develop new ideas, make proposals, re-align work flow or solve problems. Involvement is key to enriching a job.

- Assign a new or special project that will stretch their skills.

- Place the employee in a new work team. Let them do another job for awhile. This may uncover new talents while keeping them inspired.

- Cross-train employees in areas outside their normal functions — even if you don't need the coverage at the time. The opportunity helps them feel like their skills are being fully developed.

- Involve the employee in interviewing or hiring decisions.

Jesse looked it over carefully and asked, "What if your employee doesn't want to be on a new team? Or what if they don't want to take on new responsibilities?"

"Then don't," Cynthia answered. "The key is to ascertain the employee's interests *before* making any changes."

"You know the common theme that I see in your job enrichment techniques?" Jesse posed with a confident tone.

"What's that?" asked Cynthia, smiling back.

"Involvement," answered Jesse. "One of the reasons that your company is so good at keeping better employees is because you involve them in more than just the job."

Cynthia liked Jesse's astute conclusions and she knew that he was on the right path to becoming a People Keeper himself. "You're right, involvement plugs them into the company's progress and success in as many ways as possible — and that creates cohesion," Cynthia said. "One thing that's critical to understand about top performers is that most consider close involvement absolutely necessary to personal job satisfaction and dedication. Knowing that, why wouldn't a company want to find more ways to involve good employees?"

"I'm going to speculate on that," said Jesse. "I know many managers who think that they're supposed to have all the answers, so going to employees for input would be a sign of weakness."

"You've got it," declared Cynthia. "Some managers have a difficult time admitting that an employee thought up an idea or solution that they hadn't thought of themselves."

"Maybe it's a threat to a manager's ego," Jesse mused. "By the way, how did you become such a believer in this employee involvement stuff?"

"Sawyer, of course," Cynthia replied. "How else do you think 'Brash Cindy' would let go of her power center?" Cynthia chuckled and Jesse joined in, seeing her point. "First, he helped me understand that the advantages to employee involvement are enormous."

"What kind of advantages?" asked Jesse, wanting to make sure he got it too.

"That's easy," answered Cynthia. "First, solutions or changes are implemented quicker because employees are in on the discussions — so you don't have to spend a lot of time convincing them to take action. Second, you get higher quality decisions because so many in-house 'experts' are giving input. Third, it builds morale and commitment. We believe that people will lend their support to what they've helped create. Finally, involvement creates cohesion because it increases employee motivation and job satisfaction."

Jesse completed a quick note as Cynthia finished. "Sawyer taught me something a few years ago that just came to me," she said.

*A People Keeper
is wise enough to know enough
to not know too much.*

"What Sawyer was saying, of course, is that a People Keeper is confident enough to admit that they need help and asks for input from employees. He taught me that a People Keeper strongly avoids looking like a know-it-all. If you work for Sawyer, you'll find that he seldom tells you what he thinks until he's heard everyone's opinion."

"Why does he do that?" Jesse wanted to know.

"What kind of input do you think he'd get from managers and employees if he conveyed his thoughts on something first?"

Jesse thought about that and said, "Probably a lot of agreement and not much else."

"You're right," Cynthia acknowledged.

"Sawyer is really something else, isn't he?" Jesse said.

"He sure is," said Cynthia. "Those of us who are fortunate enough to work here get used to his style of getting employees involved. As Sawyer often says to managers, 'Being a great People Keeper requires that you involve employees in the company while involving yourselves with employees.'"

"No wonder you have a waiting list of employees wanting to work here," remarked Jesse.

"Thank you, but we're not without our challenges," Cynthia responded. "In fact, we've made some real changes around here in the last two years to better compete for talent and motivate our employees."

"Like what?" Jesse questioned, surprised that Sawyer's company had experienced challenges with the scarcity of quality employees.

"For example, we use employee-centered job features more than ever," answered Cynthia. "We have to make the work-place satisfying and up tempo for our better employees if we expect to prosper in the future."

"I'd like some examples of your employee-centered job enhancements," requested Jesse.

"Okay," Cynthia said. She stood and walked to the marker board at the front of the room. "First, tell me what you think are the most significant factors impacting an employer today, then we'll look at some specific enhancements that we use here."

Jesse and Cynthia came up with a list together:

FACTORS IMPACTING
WHAT EMPLOYERS PROVIDE
■■■■■■■■■■■■■■■■■■■■■■

- Employees want more control over their work schedules.

- Employees have pressing needs away from work (i.e. childcare, family concerns, children's activities.)

- Employees lead very busy personal lives and want help balancing work demands with personal time requirements.

- Employees may value the rewards *from* work over the rewards of work. This means that the fulfillment and challenge of the job may be more attractive than making better money elsewhere.

- Employees may be interested in working from their home.

- Better employees are difficult to attract and keep.

"Good job!" Cynthia praised as she returned to her seat. "You have some great insight on this already."

"Thanks," Jesse responded. "But as an employer, where do you begin to address these factors and compete with hiring and keeping employees?"

"Simple, you start by dialoguing with your employees about what they want," responded Cynthia. "Find out what they'd like, and then do what's within your means. If you develop employee-centered job enhancements that have high perceived value to employees, you'll be able to compete for the best employees out there."

"So that starts with learning what your employees would like," said Jesse. "I see how that makes sense. But tell me, what are some of the employee-centered job enhancements that you offer?"

Cynthia gave Jesse a guide used at Sawyer's company:

EMPLOYEE-CENTERED
JOB ENHANCEMENTS
▪▪▪▪▪▪▪▪▪▪▪▪▪▪▪▪

• Flexible scheduling. Stagger employee hours to accommodate personal needs, i.e. children's activities, hobbies, recreation. Or post the hours you need filled and allow employees to choose the hours they'd like to work.

• Discretionary days off. These days are awarded to employees for accomplishments, or for years/ months of service. The employee may use them for whatever reason they want.

• Fridays off early. Once every two weeks, we allow half of our support and hourly staff to leave three hours early if all work goals for the week are complete. They decide and manage their own time to be able to do that, like staying late a few days, or taking half of the lunch break, etc.

• Telecommuting. About 20 percent of our employees are allowed to work at least part-time from home. More may be allowed to do so in the future as we assess its effectiveness.

• Family-friendly features. Some considerations for child care, maternity/paternity leave, elder care and even pet care may be available.

"Now please understand that what we offer is a direct result of what we learned that our better employees want and what fits within our budget," Cynthia stated. "There's probably a better way for you to address your company's needs."

"Yeah, but this is a good start," Jesse said as he looked over the list. He thought about one of his better employees who left a year ago. She wanted more flexibility in her schedule so that she could be home at the end of the school day. She left when her needs weren't met, and her skills, years of experience, and exceptional attitude walked out the door with her.

Only now did Jesse realize just how much it had cost him to lose her — hiring costs, training time and expense, using more than one employee to cover the responsibilities that she handled alone — that single loss was incalculable, he thought.

Cynthia noticed that Jesse was deep in thought, "Mulling that over, are you?"

"Oh yes," Jesse replied, startled. "What if your employees take advantage of you on these things?"

"You mean for example, what if they use the time off for something else than what was intended?" asked Cynthia.

Jesse nodded.

"You're worried over nothing," Cynthia said. "The chances of a better employee doing that is very minimal. There's a much greater likelihood that you'll have a more appreciative and motivated employee who will stay with you because they realize what you've done to keep them. Now that doesn't mean that you should give these liberties without stipulations, because that would invite problems. What you should do is explain what's expected when they leave work early or follow a more flexible schedule."

"But how do you know for sure that your efforts as a People Keeper, and that providing employee-centered benefits are strong enough enrichments to keep better employees from leaving?" Jesse probed.

"Excellent question," Cynthia praised. "Just consider how much is at stake if you invest your efforts in being a People Keeper but they fall short and better employees still leave — a situation you could have prevented if only you had known what to do."

"I want to avoid that," responded Jesse. "How do you monitor the effectiveness of your efforts here?"

"With the People Keeper Survey," Cynthia answered. "Have you heard about it yet?"

"No, what is it?" asked Jesse.

"Here's a copy to take with you," responded Cynthia as she swivelled her chair around to a filing cabinet and retrieved a copy for Jesse.

THE PEOPLE KEEPER SURVEY

Scale: *Very Satisfied, Satisfied, Don't Know, Dissatisfied, Very Dissatisfied*

1. I am provided with adequate training and development opportunities for growth.

2. My job provides adequate advancement opportunities.

3. My job gives me sufficient challenge and fulfillment.

4. I am satisfied with my current job and am not looking for other job opportunities outside the company.

5. Coming to work is a positive experience.

6. The atmosphere is relaxed enough for me to enjoy the work.

7. I am provided with the right resources in order to do my job with excellence and timeliness.

8. I am given enough autonomy that I don't feel like I have to always send it "upstairs" before taking action.

9. Work safety is important to the company.

10. My immediate manager provides an appropriate amount of communication and feedback related to my job.

11. My immediate manager is good about training and coaching me in ways to improve my performance.

12. My immediate manager gives me an appropriate amount of praise and/or recognition when I do an excellent job.

13. My immediate manager appreciates the contribution I make to the work here.

14. I am satisfied with the way my immediate manager listens and carefully considers my ideas or concerns.

15. I am treated with respect by my immediate manager.

16. My immediate manager is available most of the time when I need to ask a question or get help.

17. My immediate manager does a good job of recognizing and celebrating team accomplishments.

18. There is an appropriate level of cooperation *between* teams in the company.

19. In my area people cooperate and work together well to accomplish goals.

20. My morale is at an appropriate level.

21. My immediate manager has made the goals for our team clear.

22. I understand clearly what is expected of me and my role in the company's success.

23. I feel that my immediate manager makes my personal job satisfaction a high enough priority.

24. My immediate manager cares about my success here.

25. In my area there is appropriate open communication.

26. There is a satisfactory level of trust in my area.

27. Upper leadership properly values my function and contribution to the organization.

28. Overall, I am compensated fairly for the work I do.

29. I plan to continue working here for the next 12 months.

30. I would recommend the company as an employer to my friends or family.

"The thing I want you to see is that the survey is a great way for us to measure the level of employee job satisfaction company-wide," Cynthia said. "It's also a measurement for how well we're doing at being People Keepers."

"I've never measured employee job satisfaction," admitted Jesse. "I guess I'm wondering whether it's really necessary as long as you develop a positive relationship with your employees?"

"You must be kidding!" responded Cynthia. "Measuring effectiveness is key to improving as a People Keeper. Sawyer has a principle he emphasizes with us quite often:

*The most important question
you can get in the habit
of asking an employee is:*

How well are we doing?

"What kind of improvement can you expect to make in employee motivation and retention if you *don't* objectively and regularly measure effectiveness?" asked Cynthia.

"I see that now, but don't you wonder whether a manager is taking this seriously enough?" Jesse asked.

"They do when they get the results," chuckled Cynthia. "If a manager gets a low score on being a People Keeper, then we coach them back up to excellence. Since the scoring is done anonymously by the employees, no one has reason for not accepting feedback."

"How long do you let poor scores as a People Keeper go on before you take further action?" Jesse asked with curiosity.

"I can't answer that," Cynthia said. "It varies with the person and the situation. But sometimes we go visit with the employees in a small group and try to discover how to best help the manager. Since the employees know that their input is to help, not hurt the manager, they're usually willing to offer beneficial ideas."

"Your managers aren't threatened by that?" asked Jesse.

"No, but they are curious and sometimes even a little worried," answered Cynthia. "You see, a People Keeper wants to improve, and we all have some improvement to make. Our managers know that it's being done to help them, not weed them out. The main goal is to improve job satisfaction and motivation for our employees. This tool gives us an opportunity to intervene when it's necessary to steer someone back on course. We've saved a number of good People Keepers and employees over the years by using the survey wisely."

"I have one more question for you," Jesse said. "How often do you use this survey?"

"Once annually for everyone," Cynthia responded. "But for new managers or for one with low scores on a previous survey, we use it twice annually. This allows us to help new managers develop the core People Keeper skills during their critical first year. And we can stay on top of the improvement efforts of those needing additional coaching."

Jesse stood and started to thank Cynthia for her help.

"Now before we finish up, there's something you need to know," Cynthia continued. "I've had an unusual request from some of the employees who found out that you and I were meeting."

"What do you mean?" Jesse asked as he sat back down.

"Well, a group of employees are assembling in the conference room once we're done," Cynthia explained. "They want to share something with you and I told them I thought it would be great if you heard it directly from them."

Jesse said goodbye and walked down the familiar hallway.

CHAPTER EIGHT

Being A Role Model And Mentor

Three employees were already seated around the conference table. Jesse smiled and introduced himself, eager to learn why they wanted to speak to him.

"Mr. Shands, we're delighted that you're here learning how to be a People Keeper," announced Ken, who had been with the service department for nearly three decades. "But we wanted to speak with you because we want to caution you."

That alarmed Jesse and his smile turned to a serious look.

"Others just like you have come here to learn about being People Keepers, but they left disappointed," Ken continued. "They viewed this as a management seminar or another business fad. They weren't really serious about changing their company to become a First-Choice Employer."

"But we hear that you're different," said Julie. She was unafraid to speak up, something she'd been doing in the data processing department for ten years. "Is it true that you're determined to make this work for your company?"

"Yes," Jesse said confidently. "I *am* going to be a People Keeper, my managers *will* be People Keepers, and our company *will* become a First-Choice Employer. I'd welcome any suggestions you have for a head start on becoming a People Keeper."

"Sure," Hamp replied. He was a stocky man who worked in customer service and planned to retire in about eight years. "Your top priority should be to build positive relationships and to be a mentor to your employees. The difference in Sawyer's company compared to other places that I've worked, is that our managers care about us and they constantly show it."

"Caring about the employee is key to creating a positive relationship and being a role model to employees," Julie said.

"I agree wholeheartedly," Hamp remarked. "Caring is an action here, not just a word. If what you need is a little praise or encouragement you get it. But if what you need is correction, you get that too. Call it tough love if you want, but we know without a doubt that they really care about us as people."

"Normally, you don't think of caring in context with the rough, fast-paced business world," Ken said. "But you should, and if more companies did they'd be First-Choice Employers just like Sawyer. He's the most caring man I've ever worked for."

"What does he do that makes you feel that way?" Jesse wondered.

"For one thing, he still sends a personally signed birthday card to each employee," Julie said.

"And he makes it a point to get around and talk with employees in all areas of the company," said Ken. "That's the best possible way for him to invest his time."

"Why?" asked Jesse.

"Have you ever heard of the ripple effect?" asked Julie, smiling.

Jesse nodded, smiling back.

"Well, it spills over and affects our managers, who communicate with employees better here than in any company I've ever seen," Julie responded.

"Added to that is the fact that Sawyer's example of caring has trickled down to the managers who care for the employees, and the employees who care about this company," Hamp said. "One of his favorite sayings is displayed on banners throughout the company that says:

The People Keeper's Pledge:

Whatever you see me do, do it too!

"Sawyer believes that every People Keeper should be able to say that to their employees," Hamp continued. "Sawyer believes that if employees have good mentor-managers, they will be more motivated and dedicated to do the right things every day."

"I'm not a very religious person, but I like Sawyer's talks that he gives each quarter," Julie said quietly. "In the last one, he talked about great leaders, and he spoke about Jesus. He said Jesus believed that the best leader was the one who focused on serving others, not on being served. Sawyer told us that we all could benefit by thinking of ways to serve each other. That attitude permeates this company, and it's one of the reasons people stay."

Ken leaned in a little closer and locked his eyes with Jesse's. "My manager used to be a real you-know-what, but you'd never know it now," he said. "He's one of the nicest people you could ever meet. Before Sawyer got a hold of him, he was hard to work for and real critical. Now Rudy is one of the nicest People Keepers in the company, a real gem. I consider him a mentor, not just my boss."

Jesse's jaw dropped a few inches. "Rudy?" he gasped.

"Yes, Rudy," answered Ken, smiling.

"Sawyer is amazing," Jesse said. "He has such an impact on people."

The employees stood to leave when they'd said their piece. Jesse thanked them for their time but remained in the conference room to reflect. He felt encouraged because the employees showed an interest in his success. He was beginning to understand that a People Keeper has the opportunity to powerfully influence the lives of others. It was exciting, and he felt even more committed now to seeing that every employee in his company is working for a People Keeper.

He finished a few more notes from his visit with the employees and then left for the hotel. After he read the Fifth Tenet, Jesse turned off the light and wondered what secrets he would discover tomorrow.

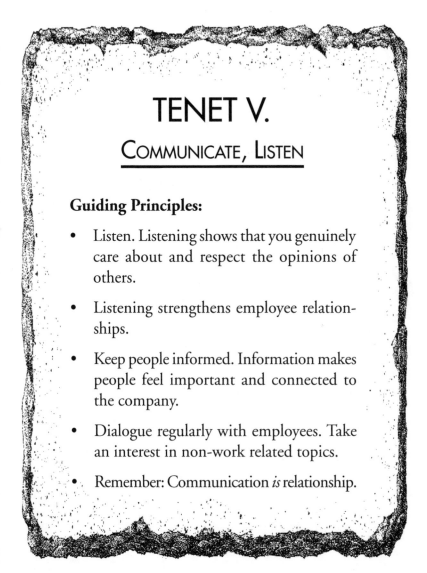

TENET V.

COMMUNICATE, LISTEN

Guiding Principles:

- Listen. Listening shows that you genuinely care about and respect the opinions of others.

- Listening strengthens employee relationships.

- Keep people informed. Information makes people feel important and connected to the company.

- Dialogue regularly with employees. Take an interest in non-work related topics.

- Remember: Communication *is* relationship.

CHAPTER NINE

The Fifth Tenet
Communicate, Listen

Jesse read the Fifth Tenet again the next day before heading to Sawyer's company.

He wondered who would help him with the Fifth Tenet. "Why not gather a mixed group of managers and employees?" he thought. He called ahead and arranged to meet the customer service manager, the retail merchandise manager, and one employee from each of these departments.

Jesse knocked on the closed door to Harold Gilming's office, and the customer service manager told him to come on in. Jesse shook hands with Harold, a husky fellow with broad shoulders. "It's great to meet you, Mr. Shands," Harold said.

"I really appreciate you taking the time to arrange this meeting," said Jesse.

The rest of the group assembled and introduced themselves to Jesse, who then said, "I'd like to know why the Fifth Tenet is so important to being a People Keeper?"

"Because employees want regular dialogue with their manager," said Jerry Fine, retail merchandise manager.

Jesse looked in the direction of Mylene Sanders, a 12-year veteran with the company. She was a chipper and energetic brunette who seemed eager to speak. "Our company wants its managers to develop positive relationships with employees, and communication is the best way to do that," she said. "How can you build a positive relationship with someone who you don't have good communication with?"

"Right," Jesse said. "How successful can a People Keeper be if they aren't willing to spend time listening and dialoguing with employees?"

"Exactly," Mylene continued. "That's why we believe that positive relationships are built on our communication. When relationship suffers between a manager and an employee, bank on the fact that the communication has problems."

Mark Wilson, a tall young man in his late twenties, Harold's assistant team leader, said, "That's true, and let me add something. My manager, Harold, is one of the best communicators in the company. He told me that good communication comes in three forms: *chats*, *updates*, and *instruction*."

"Wow," Harold chuckled. "I said that?"

Jesse was curious now and asked, "Can you explain the three forms of communication and why they work?"

"Sure," Mark answered. "*Chats* are the art of making meaningful conversation with your employees about what they did over the weekend, the latest big movie, or how their kid's soccer game came out. It's talking about relational stuff that's not always work-related."

"The reason that's important is because it makes you feel like they take a personal interest in you," Mylene added. "Why would anyone want to stay working for a boss who shows little interest in their goals, or their life outside of work?"

"They wouldn't, of course," answered Jesse. "But aren't most of the conversations between managers and employees work-related versus non-work related?"

"Definitely," Harold replied. "An important part of our chats with employees is to use a manager's tool called the Power of 12. Its purpose is to help People Keepers stay in touch with their employees' feelings regarding work-related issues. You might say it's a gauge, a way to keep your finger on the pulse."

"But how does a busy People Keeper stay involved with employees without spending an inordinate amount of time?" asked Jesse.

"That's the beauty of this tool, it doesn't have to take a lot of time to use it effectively," answered Harold as he passed a copy to Jesse.

THE POWER OF 12
■■■■■■■■■■■■■■

1. What 3 things do you like about working here?

2. What 3 things disappoint or frustrate you about working here?

3. What 3 goals will you be working on over the next 90 days?

4. List 3 ways that I as your manager, can help make your job more meaningful, rewarding, or challenging?

"Look at it as a vehicle for getting quick, regular employee feedback," explained Harold. "Every 90 days with new employees the People Keeper gets answers to questions like these. We use it less frequently with long-term employees, but at least once annually for everyone."

"Why is it called the Power of 12?" asked Jesse.

"Four questions, three responses each," Mark replied. "But we don't insist on three responses, just like we don't insist on just these four questions. Each People Keeper is encouraged to start with these but also come up with questions that best fit their situation. For example, here are two other questions that Harold and I use with our direct reports:

- What are we *not* doing currently that could make a difference in how long you'd stay, if we started doing it?

- What 3 new duties or responsibilities would you like to be trained on in the near future?"

"Those are great questions that I'd like to use," Jesse said smiling. "But what I'd really like to know is why the Power of 12 works so well?"

"Before I answer that, let me ask you a question," Mark replied. "Would you prefer to discover that one of your better employees was disenchanted about their job *before* or *after* they decide to leave?"

"Who wouldn't want to know before?" replied Jesse.

"Right," Harold remarked. "The Power of 12 allows a People Keeper to find out before a loss happens."

"But aren't some of these potentially risky questions?" Jesse probed, still surprised by the willingness of Sawyer's company to open up with employees.

Harold shook his head and answered, "No, there's greater risk if you don't ask questions like these. Do you think that by keeping an issue buried it goes away? Don't issues grow or multiply if they go unattended?"

Mylene sat straight up. "I like the Power of 12 because it gives me a chance to let my boss know where my head is at," she said. "If I want, I can get something out in the open that I'm peeved about – which isn't very often around here, but it does happen. My boss is great to talk with me about any concerns that I have. At least I know that he cares about my goals and about me as a member of this team. If they didn't have the Power of 12, a lot of issues would get bottled up inside employees, and management would miss out on valuable feedback."

"It's not just about problems though," said Jerry. "Notice that the tool also deals with what the employee likes, and what their goals are. Also, I use questions similar to Harold's and Mark's that ask the employee to tell me what new projects or tasks they'd like to try. These discussions help immensely to keep the employee's job challenging and rewarding."

Jesse could see that the Power of 12 had quite an impact on Sawyer's company. He recognized that getting problems out in the open was key to avoiding job dissatisfaction. "Even if it's uncomfortable to talk about, you have an open door policy, don't you?" he asked.

"Correct," Jerry said. "For example, even if an employee expresses concerns about pay or a situation in which they felt unfairly treated, we discuss it. By getting it out in the open you can deal with it effectively. Isn't it better to deal with a possible shortcoming now than to deal with a two-week notice later? When you use a tool like the Power of 12, it says to your employees that you care about them and you're interested in their success."

"Right," Jesse agreed. "But won't it be embarrassing or threatening to the leader?"

"You mean threaten their ego?" Jerry quizzed. "A People Keeper checks their ego at the front door. Isn't it true that to improve at anything you must first admit that there's a problem or shortcoming?"

"Right again," replied Jesse. "Okay, now tell me about updates and why they work."

"*Updates* keep you current on relevant issues and they make you feel like you're an important part of this company," Mark replied.

"I think what you see in many other organizations is an attitude from ownership or management that they can't trust their employees with information," Harold said. "Or they assume that sharing information will create more problems than keeping it undisclosed. People Keepers, on the other hand, include employees in what's going on using regular updates, such as our weekly departmental meetings."

"Why is it important to have weekly meetings?" Jesse wondered.

"A weekly meeting gives employees information that is important to their job, like updates on our company or department goals," Jerry said. "We also review a new project, present the results of an employee survey, or discuss customer feedback. It's an opportunity to bring everyone back together to focus on what's important to us at that time, like production, sales, or quality measures. In addition, meetings offer information that gives employees a lit path — knowing what's expected and where we're headed prepares employees for our expectations so they can produce better results."

"Jesse, let me use an illustration that gives you an example of what we're saying in a visual way," Harold stated. "Shut your eyes and place your hands over them."

Jesse placed his pen and notebook aside and went along. The room was now pitch dark to him.

"Now, let's say your goal is to get up and with your eyes closed, go touch a green dot that we've placed somewhere in this room," Harold continued.

Jesse started to get up when Harold said, "No, we're just kidding, don't get up, but keep your eyes covered. If we did ask you to do this how hard do you think it would be to find that green dot?"

"Very difficult, because I can't see where I'm going," Jesse answered.

"Exactly," Harold affirmed. "And how long do you think it would take you to complete that goal, if you could at all?"

"A long time," Jesse replied. "I'd be moving very slowly since I'd have to feel my way around the room touching everything until you told me that I'd found it."

"That's exactly how an employee feels when they're kept in the dark," Harold said. "They never really feel connected to what's going on. Around here we believe that feeling informed plays a big role in feeling a valuable part of the team. What do you think occurs from keeping employees in a dim pathway?"

"They experiment a lot, which leads to more mistakes and much slower progress," Jesse answered. "Or, I guess the dim pathway could freeze the progress of some employees so that they hardly risk doing anything that might be wrong, they probably just do enough to get by."

"Precisely," said Harold. "By the way, go ahead and open your eyes now." Harold smiled and waited a moment for Jesse's eyes to adjust to the light again. "Now, suppose that we asked you to find the green dot with your eyes open, how quickly could you do it?"

Jesse glanced around the room and was shocked to see a green dot on the corner of the flip chart by Harold's desk. He jumped up and touched it.

Everyone in the room exploded in laughter and applause.

Jesse returned to his seat smiling and said, "That was a great illustration. What employee could stay motivated and highly productive if they worked for a manager that kept them in the dark on things?"

"You've got that right," Mylene spoke up. "The most my previous employer did to communicate with employees was to post announcements and the mission statement on a bulletin board. No explanation was really given, and when we did have meetings they were usually to harp on something that they wanted done."

The three managers nodded.

"You tested me, now let me try you guys on something," Jesse said. "Take a sheet of paper and list the mission and the main goals of your company."

A very brief moment passed before all four employees

scooted their sheets across the table. Jesse glanced at the pages. "I can't believe this," he said. "Your answers are all the same! I didn't think everyone would know this — especially you, Mylene."

"Gee, thanks," Mylene said, not sure what Jesse meant by that.

"No offense meant," Jesse quickly said when he realized how she took his declaration. "I just didn't think that a non-management employee would know this about the company. It's obvious to me that Sawyer is serious about communication."

"Yes, he's very committed," said Harold. "Sawyer believes that a First-Choice Employer communicates to employees the goals, their values, why they do it and who they do it for. He believes that we update employees thoroughly and often. Sawyer taught me a principle when I became a People Keeper that really helped me grasp the significance of employee communication:

'Employees won't know the importance of
their roles until your role is the employee's importance.'"

"What's that have to do with communication?" Jesse asked.

"Everything!" Harold answered. "A significant component of effective communication is conveying to the employee that their individual contribution is essential to the company's success."

"Everyone wants to be needed and everyone needs to be wanted," Jesse said. "Is that what you're saying?"

"Yes," replied Harold. "A People Keeper must make an employee feel needed or important. Accordingly, being included in vital information about the company contributes to one's dedication."

"Right," Jesse said. "In the absence of being well informed, I'll bet many hourly employees just treat their responsibilities like another j-o-b."

"If more companies communicated like Sawyer and our managers do, they wouldn't have such negative employees," Mylene remarked.

"What does negativity have to do with communication?" Jesse asked, wanting to make sure that he understood.

"A lot," answered Mylene. "What do you think happens when employees exist in a vacuum, out of the loop as far as company information goes?"

"They start creating communication on their own?" Jesse probed.

"Definitely," Mylene replied. "And then the company grapevine really gets revved up. You see, when employees lack information, the grapevine just fuels their negativity and suspicions — and trust may break down, too."

"I can see that," said Jesse. "So chats and updates are tools that a People Keeper uses to communicate with employees. These tools help maintain positive relations and trust, two important keys to retaining better employees."

The four employees agreed completely with Jesse's assessment. "Can you tell me now how a People Keeper uses instruction?" Jesse wanted to learn.

"It's used in two ways," Mark said. "*Instruction* means that you make your expectations crystal clear. Instruction also means that you explain how you want the work completed. Did you know that over 80 percent of business problems or mistakes can be attributed to a failure to communicate?"

"No," Jesse said, a little startled. "Are most companies filled with such poor communicators?"

"Yes, most are mediocre," Harold answered. "Stop and think about all the mistakes, errors, omissions, reworks, misunderstandings and negative feelings that occur in the workplace. A surprising number of those come from shortcomings in a manager's communication. Now People Keepers aren't perfect communicators, but we have learned how to drastically reduce the most common communication mistakes, and make our company a better place to work. Would you like to know our secret?"

"Of course," Jesse said with anticipation.

Mark handed Jesse a copy of the reminder tool.

How To Instruct Employees and Eliminate Under-Communication
■■■■■■■■■■■■■■■■■■■■■■■■■■■■■

- Give the employee reasons why the task is important and relevant to them.

- Explain how it will positively impact them if they act on this information appropriately.

- Explain what will be expected of them and how their work will be evaluated.

- Tell them when you want the work completed and where they can go if they need help.

"When you provide these four components of instruction, you avoid about 95 percent of communication mistakes," Jerry remarked.

Jesse was studying the list, realizing that he could use these techniques with his own managers to improve his own communication. He also remembered many instances when a manager had misunderstood Jesse's instructions, or they simply didn't follow through on it as quickly as he'd intended.

"Now we must move on to listening," Harold said, interrupting Jesse's thoughts.

"Right," Mylene replied, smiling. "We're not letting you leave until we tell you the secrets of the forgotten side of communication."

"Why is listening so important to being a People Keeper?" Jesse asked.

"Listening says that you care about that person, and it says that you respect them," Jerry said. "Can you think of two more powerful messages to send to an employee you want to keep?"

"No," answered Jesse.

"Jesse, who were some of the best listeners in your personal or work life?" asked Jerry.

"Sawyer comes to mind, and my wife," Jesse said.

"Did listening impact the quality of your relationships with these two individuals?" Jerry probed.

"Yes, in many ways," remarked Jesse. "You can't have a positive relationship with someone unless they're a good listener, can you?"

"It's not impossible, but it will be very difficult," Jerry answered. "Listening will either be a bridge or a barricade to relationships. Listening is a choice, you either choose to listen or you choose to tune someone out."

"I agree," added Mylene, "I used to work directly for Jerry and I must say, he was a fantastic listener."

"Why?" Jesse said as he flipped his notebook to a new sheet of paper.

"Because he wanted to," Mylene said. "I think that over half of what makes a good listener is the 'want to'. With Jerry, you get the feeling that what you have to say is important to him. Unless he's really tied up with something he'll put aside his work and hear you out."

"Do good listeners just come by it naturally?" Jesse was curious.

"No," Jerry said. "Look, my wife and kids can tell you that until I started working for Sawyer, I was a terrible listener. I was impatient, I interrupted people, and I tried to get two other things done while I listened. Also, if they didn't get to the point quickly enough for me, I'd hurry them along rather abruptly."

"What did you do to get so good at listening?" asked Jesse.

"I owe it all to Sawyer," Jerry answered. "In helping me to become a People Keeper he taught me his four helpful listening rules." As he handed another reminder tool to Jesse, he added, "You know how Sawyer has a knack of coming up with memorable tips that are so easy to use with people."

Jesse nodded, smiling as he read the listening rules:

E.A.R.S. For Listening

Engage–get others talking. Remember, you don't learn from talking, only by listening.

Ask–ask questions to show an interest and to confirm that you understand what they're trying to get across. *Say*: What did you mean by that? Why do you feel that way? How would that work? What solutions have you come up with?

Respect–consider other people's opinions and ideas as important and valid as your own. Remember, you never know where the best solution or idea may come from.

Sincere–take a sincere interest in the other person's message, only then will you give your undivided attention. Concentrate 100 percent on what the other person is trying to convey to you. Don't interrupt.

"If you're finished with us, I understand that Sawyer would like to meet with you in a couple of hours," Harold said suddenly, noticing that Jesse had just finished reading the reminder tool. "He came back a little early from his fishing trip and he's excited about visiting with you."

"Great," remarked Jesse. He looked forward to getting with Sawyer too.

Jesse thanked the employees for the valuable insights that he had gained about communication and listening. He then caught the elevator down to the first floor, still reflecting on the remarkable, yet practical ways that the People Keeper develops positive relationships with employees.

CHAPTER TEN

Reward And Appreciation In Action

Jesse looked for a coffee shop as soon as he left Sawyer's building. He wanted to be alone for a couple of hours and look over his rapidly-expanding notebook.

Out of the corner of his eye he noticed a limousine headed in his direction. As it slowed to a stop, six ladies from Sawyer's clerical team filed out the door, giggling and smiling. The ladies were awed by the sight of the limousine.

"Now you honored ladies get in before the driver leaves you here!" said an older gentleman as he held the door for the group. His jesting was instantly met with more girlish giggles as the ladies climbed gleefully into the black superstretch limo.

"What's this for?" Jesse asked.

"They've been awarded a limousine ride to a luncheon at a nice restaurant," he said.

"For what?" Jesse asked, the curiosity too much to restrain.

The man didn't seem to mind and introduced himself as the company's administrative manager. He explained that Sawyer's company wanted a way to reward the ladies for their continued teamwork and the extra effort they'd given recently to a special rush project.

The limo pulled away as the joyous rattle coming from the back seat intensified. Those ladies will remember the gratitude that the company had demonstrated for a long time to come, Jesse thought. A genuine compliment, praise or reward really *can* create a lasting memory. Sawyer and his company never ceased to amaze Jesse.

When the time came he walked to the other end of the building and took the stairs to Sawyer's office.

CHAPTER ELEVEN

The People Keeper's Action Plan

When Jesse walked in Sawyer was enjoying photos of his fishing trip. "Jesse, come on in, it's great to see you," Sawyer said as he put the pictures aside. "Hey, do you want to see my catch?"

"Sure," Jesse answered, glad to see his friend so excited. Sawyer proudly handed the pictures to Jesse one by one, explaining the significance of each scene and each catch.

"Well, enough of that," Sawyer announced as he placed the pictures back in their folder and sat down slowly. "What do you think — do you still want to be a People Keeper?"

"Absolutely!" Jesse said. "I discovered the secrets of keeping better employees satisfied and motivated. Now I know that my company can become a team of People Keepers and a First-Choice Employer just like yours."

"Splendid," responded Sawyer. "I'll bet you're leaving with a satchel full of reminder tools, aren't you?"

"Yes, a satchel full," Jesse chuckled.

"Jesse, listen carefully," Sawyer said, suddenly becoming serious. "Here's the most important question that I have for you — why does the People Keeper work?"

"There are two reasons why the People Keeper works so well," Jesse told his old friend. "First, the People Keeper focuses on developing a positive relationship with employees. It's clear to me now that work relations between a manager and an employee are critical to keeping better employees. Second, the People Keeper works because it's a well thought-out strategy. Each tenet is a simple, yet highly effective method for getting the most out of a person while keeping them satisfied."

"Wonderful answer," Sawyer responded with much delight. "I'm impressed with your efforts this week, Jesse."

"Thank you," responded Jesse. "But do you have an action plan for implementing the People Keeper in an organization? I could use a quick start."

"Yes, we do," Sawyer acknowledged. "That is if you have room in that satchel of yours for one more reminder tool!"

Sawyer handed the action plan to Jesse:

THE PEOPLE KEEPER'S ACTION PLAN

1. Make a list of the areas that you want to work on personally.

2. Plan to implement a few of the ideas each week by marking them in your planner-scheduler.

3. Review one of the tenets each week for 10 weeks. You'll come up with more ideas and insights this way.

4. Get at least one other manager to partner with you in applying the People Keeper.

5. Administer the People Keeper Survey and act on any weaknesses immediately.

6. Begin to make notes of the changes you see in your employees and your organization.

7. Invest in others. Give the gift of the People Keeper to someone you'd like to see increase their success.

"Again, the greatest single action you can take is in being a mentor-teacher," Sawyer emphasized. "Being an effective People Keeper begins with you."

No one questioned the impact Sawyer had made as a mentor on countless others both within and outside his company.

"Jesse," Sawyer said, breaking the silence, "you will have a much greater impact on people than I've had."

Jesse started to interrupt. "But…"

"No, no," insisted Sawyer. "In my dreams I've seen you multiply the People Keeper's reach so that executives, managers, business owners, clergy, administrators and government leaders everywhere benefit from its ancient wisdom.

"Listen to me, I'm an old man now and the People Keeper needs a younger man like you to spread the secrets of the ancient tablet. When the time comes, you will write a book — this too I have seen in my dreams. Jesse, I believe that you are the one whom I've prayed would come along and be *the* People Keeper."

This revelation stunned but also pleased Jesse. He looked up and riveted his eyes with Sawyers and said, "I'd be honored to help others learn the secrets of the People Keeper."

Jesse's answer made Sawyer very happy. He rose and walked over to where Jesse sat. He placed his hand on his shoulder and prayed an ancient blessing:

*"God, greatly bless Jesse and enlarge his sphere
of influence and territory. Let your guiding hand
be with him and keep him from harm."*

Jesse received the blessing. He prospered greatly over the years as he put the People Keeper in practice. He retained a core group of experienced, talented employees — and profits skyrocketed. His company created more jobs and better employment opportunities than ever before. The company was now a respected First-Choice Employer.

The legend of the People Keeper spread quickly. So much of Jesse's time was spent coaching the managers who inquired about being a People Keeper, that he decided it was the right time for the book Sawyer had envisioned.

CHAPTER TWELVE

Anyone Can Be A People Keeper

At a cabin surrounded by the serenity of a nearby lake and the quiet of whispering oak and cedar trees, Jesse stowed away to write. His old friend had taught him that anyone could be a great People Keeper. He knew from experience that it was true, and now he wanted to convey that same promise to everyone.

Before publishing the book, Jesse gave copies of his notes to his newest managers. He was thrilled at how they applied the principles, re-read the sections that they needed to focus on, and made changes at a remarkable pace. It felt good to see employees all over the company more happy and content because they worked for People Keepers. Jesse was more excited than ever about sharing the secrets with others.

When the book was published he of course gave the first copy to Sawyer, now a very old man.

With an ear-to-ear smile, Sawyer excitedly clutched the book with his bony hands and turned to the first page. He began reading with a faint voice that seemed to get stronger with each sentence:

"The old archaeologist lingered over the hole where he'd been working on hands and knees for two days. He bent back down and gently slipped a hand underneath the heavy stone tablet..."

The End

THE PEOPLE KEEPER'S RESOURCES

Official Web Site:
www.thepeoplekeeper.com

★ **The People Keeper Book.** Bulk discounts are available for book orders of 10 copies or more. Email: info@thepeoplekeeper.com Or call 800-841-8540

★ **The People Keeper Seminar™:** Bring the enthusiasm of Mark Holmes "live" to your team and create People Keepers all over your organization, faster. For more information: http://www.thepeoplekeeper.com/resources.html

★ **2-Day MasterCoaching Program:** Become a better People Keeper, manager and motivator in two days of one-on-one coaching in the beautiful Missouri Ozarks with Mark Holmes. Includes two months of follow-up coaching and access to Mark. There is a less intense, quite flexible option called: People Keeper Coaching. For more information: http://www.thepeoplekeeper.com/resources.html

★ **E–People Keeper Class:** Receive a valuable system for quickly increasing employee loyalty, boosting morale, profiting from the People Keeper principles and becoming a First-Choice Employer. One 30 minute lesson is delivered to your email in-box once a week for eight weeks. Easy to use, fast and convenient and it never has to interfere with your other obligations.
For more information go to: http://www.thepeoplekeeper.com/resources.html

★ *Free* **People Keeper Survey:** Do you know how your team rates their work and workplace? Have your team answer the People Keeper Survey, and get the results, free. Find out more today, visit: http://www.thepeoplekeeper.com/resources.html

★ *Free* **People Keeper Tip of the Day on Your Web Site:** Can your web site use fresh content that will help your visitors attract, motivate and retain better employees? Then use the authentic People Keeper Tip of the Day. It's completely automated — just paste the dynamic Java applet code into your site. It's as easy as 1-2-3 and it's free! For details, visit http://www.thepeoplekeeper.com/tip.html

For More Information On Any Resource Write or Call:
The People Keeper
P.O. Box 3175, Springfield, MO 65808
Phone 800-841-8540   Fax 888-812-9631

ABOUT THE AUTHOR

Mark Holmes is a management specialist whose ideas have helped thousands of professionals at successful small businesses and multi-national corporations improve their operations with greater success and less anxiety.

His consultant activities help organizations improve performance with customers and increase teamwork, communication and leadership. Throughout his career, Holmes' ideas on employee motivation and performance have been utilized in corporations across America. He is the author of the popular *Wooing Customers Back, The Manager's Guide To Wooing Customers Back,* and numerous business articles.

Holmes is an in-demand speaker and trainer for corporations and associations. He is a member of the National Speakers Association and The Institute of Management Consultants.

He is the President of Consultant Board, Inc., which supports improved performance through consulting, training and learning materials. Holmes has put his special understanding to work with clients such as ServiceMaster Clean, Tracker Marine, Chick-fil-A and Cisco Systems , providing guidance for cultural change and better results in today's work environment.

He lives in the Ozarks of Missouri with his wife, Jeanna, and their children — Jaclyn, who is active in speech competition, and Jonathan, who plays on a basketball team Holmes helps coach. He also devotes his time to a ministry he started called Future Men In Training, meeting monthly with fathers and sons.